ALIAS BILLY THE KID
The Man Behind the Legend

Donald Cline

Sunstone Press

Santa Fe, New Mexico

Second Printing, 1986

Printed in the United States of America

Library of Congress Cataloging in Publication Data:

Cline, Donald, 1930-
    Alias Billy the Kid: the man behind the legend.

    Bibliography: p. 133
    Includes index.
    1. Billy, the Kid. 2. Outlaws--Southwest, New--
Biography. 3. Southwest, New--Biography. 4. Frontier
and pioneer life--Southwest, New. I. Title.
F786.B34C57   1986   978'.02'0924 [B]   85-26087
ISBN: 0-86534-080-3

Published in 1986 by SUNSTONE PRESS
            Post Office Box 2321
            Santa Fe, NM 87504-2321 / USA

CONTENTS

Foreword.....................................7

Special Acknowledgments......................9

1. The Birth................................11

2. The Stabbing.............................23

3. The Cahill Killing.......................46

4. Mesilla and Lincoln......................55

5. Side Lights..............................83

6. Final Days..............................103

7. Counterfeit Kids........................119

Bibliographic Sources.....................133

Index.....................................142

ILLUSTRATIONS

(Following page 92)

A young Henry McCarty (Nita Stewart Haley Library)
Lower New York City 1850
Silver City, New Mexico, circa 1915 (Twitchell Coll.)
Mogollon, New Mexico (N.M. State Records Center & Archives)
Telegram concerning the Cahill killing (U.S. Retired Military Records)
Blazer's Mill (Coll. D. Cline)
Fort Sumner in the 1870's (National Archives)
Original Army map of Fort Sumner, 1868 (National Archives)
Wortley Hotel (New Mexico Historical Society)
Pat Garrett (Museum of New Mexico, Neg. 47632)
Billy LeRoy (State Hist. Soc. of Colorado, Neg. F-5978)
William "Kid" Wilson (Coll. D. Cline)
William Cornelius (Coll. D. Cline)

FOREWORD

This book is the product of a life-long crusade spanning some thirty-five years. It became my life and my life became this book.

Of all American historical personages, more lies, misrepresentations, myths and legends have been presented than any other concerning Henry McCarty, alias William H. Bonney, alias Billy the Kid. His life was so distorted with untruths that little, if any, resemblance to his actual life remains. He was called a Robin Hood by some, a cold-blooded murderer by others. Sometimes he appears as a romantic figure led astray by circumstances of life that he could not control, sometimes a hero, sometimes just a petty outlaw. And to most he is nothing more than the product of a Madison Avenue approach to the American dollar.

Whether you know him as Henry McCarty, Henry Antrim, William H. Bonney or simply as Billy the Kid, he was a flesh and blood human possessed of mortal demons that inhabit all men.

Marshall Ashmun Upson wrote the book **The Authentic Life of Billy the Kid** for Patrick Floyd Garrett and thus gave birth to a legend with little regard for the facts. Upson, a former newspaper reporter down on his luck and out of money, saw his opportunity to regain the professional immortality and financial status that once was his. Upson knew little, if any, of Henry McCarty's early life except the rumors and hearsay which he had heard from others. He mixed this together with a little fact and the concoction became an American folk hero to unlearned eastern readers. Other stories swiftly followed, further embellishing a lowly outlaw and common murderer into the western counterpart of a Robin Hood or Zorro. From this frothy mixture came a blurry image of a young man that was destined to capture the imagination of a nation for the next hundred years. He didn't deserve it.

Until now, Henry's early childhood remained a blank in history. Many of the Prophets of Billy Bonneydom have prophesied that no further documentation on his life would be forthcoming and that much of the necessary evidence no longer existed.

Where there be prophesies they shall fail.

Upson was not a historian nor a newsman with any respect for the truth. He created a past solely for the Garrett book and the fortune he felt would soon follow. His singular work remains a classic example of past and present newspaper work and writing. He confused some of Dave Rudabaugh's early life in Kansas for that of young Henry while other segments are simply imaginative figments to make the story more saleable. Who was there to denounce him?

Immediately following Henry McCarty's death the **Wide Awake Library** prosed his life into a small fortune aided by latter day disciples which persist until this very day. Walter Noble Burns helped America discover its lost legend almost 60 years ago and opened the door for the multitudes of pulp writers to further distort the image. Although Upson's responsibility in this matter has long been known by serious historians, too many present day writers (not historians or researchers) have accepted Upson's crowings as gospel for they lacked the energy to pursue any research of their own.

It has long been known, and accepted, that Billy the Kid's name was Henry McCarty. This fact first surfaced in 1873. The name William H. Bonney was the fourth alias he used and this did not come into being until March of 1878. Even afterwards he was sometimes still referred to as Henry McCarty and Henry Antrim. This persisted up until his death on July 14, 1881.

The name of William has long been a favorite name among outlaws for some unknown reason. Perhaps the name gives them a ring of respectability. William Bonney was not the first person to use the sobriquet of Billy the Kid — he was the second. And he certainly was not the last. This has confused many writers and historians over the years.

Many popular legends, theories, myths and misrepresentations will be exploded in this book, much to the irritation of some individuals who have championed the allegation that everything about him has already been found and nothing more exists. This is false. For the past twenty or so years I have constantly found documentation that others have not found and gone away shaking their heads. Much documentation does exist and there is much more to be found.

Henry McCarty was a man of varied images. He was a killer, a gambler, singer, piano player, a user of both men and women and a coward blessed with a charming personality that he used to advantage when needed. He was a personable, well-liked young man to those he did not steal from or needed but hated by those that were outside these categories.

He was a quicksilver personality, able to quickly cross the invisible line that divides right from wrong according to the requirements of each moment. Loved by some, despised by many, hated by even more but known to all as William H. Bonney — Billy the Kid — a legend in his own time. Often controversial, always blurred, his translucent image continues to live on in film and the written word.

Here, then, is the real man . . . and the legend.

SPECIAL ACKNOWLEDGMENTS

A special acknowledgment is given to former director of the Municipal Archives and Records Center in New York, James Katsaros. Without his help as well as knowledge of the archives and early New York, this book would never have been completed. And without this help, devotion to duty and unending cooperation the light would never have shone on Henry McCarty's early life.

I would also like to thank the office of two Presidents of the United States and three U.S. Senators: Ronald Reagan, Lyndon B. Johnson, Edwin Mechem, Clinton P. Anderson and Joseph M. Montoya. Their cooperation opened political doors that might have remained shut in the Department of Immigration; Bureau of the Census; Diplomatic, Legal and Fiscal Branch; Department of the Army, Retired Military records; Department of Commerce; the Consulate General of Ireland and the National Library of Ireland located in Dublin.

A special thanks also to New Mexico State Archivist Donald Lavash and the employees of the State Archives and Records Center in Santa Fe for their time, cooperation, records and efforts, and to all those county employees who allowed me to see what they did not allow others to see.

CHAPTER 1
THE BIRTH

Of all the famous and notable figures in American history none has received more widespread and undeserving attention than William H. Bonney, better known as Billy the Kid. He is known above all our presidents and patriots to every child and adult alike. More people are familiar with his exploits, both real and imagined, through an unending flow of books and articles and, in popularity, he far exceeds that of the father of our country, George Washington.

Countless parties have made him a saintly folk hero which he decidedly does not deserve. He has been canonized in legend along with Robin Hood, Dick Turpin and Johnny Appleseed. He is engrained deeply into the western history of our country. But he was not a folk hero fighting injustices against the downtrodden nor was he a defender of right and justice. He was a personable young man who was not only a coward but a petty cattle thief who sacrificed his friends' lives in order to protect his own safety. And he preferred to live off the labor of honest men because he was unwilling to expend his own energy.

He was a liar, a thief and a user of persons. He manipulated the Governor of the Territory of New Mexico in a vain attempt to save himself by selling out his former comrades to protect his own freedom. He was a cold-blooded murderer who never risked anything. This then, is William Bonney — the man and the legend.

It has long been known, and proven, that William Bonney was born Henry McCarty and later known as Henry Antrim. Henry McCarty was born in the predominately Irish Fourth Ward section of east-side Manhattan on November 20, 1859.[1] He first saw the light of day in private furnishings at 70 Allen Street. Though he was not fortunate to have entered this world through a hospital like his older brother, Joe, they shared a common bond: they were both illegitimate.[2]

According to Joe's death certificate, he died at 76 years of age, which by my calculations, makes the year of his birth 1854. Some have tried to incorrectly state that Joe was younger than Henry but he was not. During the years 1852-1856 there was only one male child named McCarty born in the entire city of New York and that was Joseph M. McCarty. According to the birth records, he was born on August 25, 1854, at the New York Hospital located at 525 East 68th Street. Catherine McCarty is listed as the mother. No listing is given for the father.[3]

It has long been known to serious students of Billy Bonneydom that he was never William H. Bonney, Jr. with a father named William H.

Bonney, Sr. A check of the birth records from 1857-1862 disclose that no male children named Bonney were born in that city.[4] In fact, there were very few Bonneys in New York according to the records.

The New York City directories for the years 1850 through 1862 disclose that the last William Bonney was listed in that city in 1857 and none appear again until 1862. A check of all listed births during those years of every couple named Bonney show there were no male births during the years Henry and Joe were born and none had a mother named Catherine.

Over the years many searches have been made in New York through the City Clerk's (Recorder) office seeking the birth of Billy the Kid. All have been fruitless and the statement has been made too often that there is no recorded birth of William Bonney. Nothing could be further from the truth.

It has always been a requirement of law in New York that all births are recorded on their day of occurrence whether the infant had been named or not, thus a listing for Bonney exists. Secondly, none of the records are maintained in the City Clerk's office where most inquiries are directed because all records prior to 1866 are stored in the Municipal Archives and Records Center. It is here that all early births, deaths and marriages are maintained.

One writer claimed an announcement of Bonney's birth appeared in a Brooklyn newspaper while another maintained it was the **Times**. Brooklyn had no major newspapers while most were of an ethnic, trade or social origin and never printed New York births. From its inception until today, the **Times** has maintained a standard of never printing birth or death announcements unless they were people of some social standing.[5] Immigrant births and deaths were never reported.

While New York proper had many papers similar to those in Brooklyn, they had five major ones: the **Tribune, New York Times, New York Sun, The World** and **The Mercury**. All followed the prescribed pattern of births, deaths and marriages unless the individual was well-known or had some social status.

Most serious historians have never accepted the statement that William Bonney was born on November 23, 1859. The only source for this contention was the undocumented say-so of Ash Upson who created the Bonney myth for Pat Garrett in **The Authentic Life of Billy the Kid** which was not totally authentic at all.

Everyone has simply repeated much of what Upson claimed even though it was well-established among historians that Upson was wrong. (It is much easier to repeat than it is to research.)

Garrett was aware that Upson was wrong about the birthdate and he so informed Governor Miguel Otero. He said that Bonney had once told him the day but that he had forgotten. Bonney's best friend during the Lincoln County War was George Coe and Coe made the same statement as Garrett. Since two of Bonney's closest associates stated that Upson was wrong, we accept the fact that he was.

Garrett's entire book was a commercial production of Ash Upson and never intended to be a factual book of history. Upson was down on his luck and had pinned his hopes on the Garrett folklore as a way to redeem himself. This was confirmed in the various letters to his family back east.[6]

Actually, Upson was neither friend nor associate of Bonney nor did he know him well. Most of what Upson wrote was gleaned from conversations with other individuals in Lincoln or what was already printed in the papers. In some instances he mixed a small amount of fact with a lot of imagination and thereby set all future standards for works on Bonney. Most writers have simply repeated what Upson claimed, none of which had documentation. Upson did not even research the object of his pronouncements.

Upson ran a small mail service between Precinct 16 and Lincoln and from rumors, stories and conversations he formed the mythical life of Henry McCarty. Not a single one of his letters back home stated that he had ever met or knew Bonney and that he was ever in Silver City, New Mexico, has always been in doubt. There is no documentation that the Antrims ever ran a boarding house in Silver City (actually it was Mrs. R.H. Brown) and no one in Silver City could ever confirm Upson's allegations of Bonney's life there.

What he did write home was his poor financial condition which was getting worse by the minute and that he "was a loser."[7] Much of the gist of these letters centers on his complaints of being down on his luck and in dire financial straits. The Lincoln County War had been difficult for him financially and it had left him almost penniless.[8]

While Upson ran his mail service between the two localities Alexander McSween supposedly had been collecting school money for him at the rate of $15.00 per year. He had also run a mail sack for McSween for over a year. When McSween was killed in Lincoln he died owing Upson in excess of $200.[9] He complained that other men owned him money but they had fled during the Lincoln County War without having paid him. He had a lawsuit pending against one individual in Mesilla who owed him between $400 and $500. It was at this point he made the statement that he was a born loser.

"Instead of making money I have been expending," he wrote. Wealthy Captain J.C. Lea had put in a stock of his goods in the room

13

adjacent to Upson's small office and asked Upson to watch over it. He did not pay Upson for this service but offered him board only to watch over the stock. Upson informed his relatives that he had written every word of Garrett's book for him and that he expected the monetary gains therefrom would finally remove him from his debtor's category. But the book proved to be a financial catastrophe.

Upson had once been a successful newspaper man before entering New Mexico but he was still confident that he would some day regain past glories. He constantly wrote articles to the **Times** in New York as well as the **Daily New Mexican** in Santa Fe, **The Optic** in Las Vegas, New Mexico, and possibly the **Thirty-Four** in Las Cruces, New Mexico. He often submitted these articles under fictitious names. Like all newspaper men, past and present, he was often hard-pressed for news at times and during these slack periods was prone to create the news. He followed this pattern in the early parts of the Garrett book.

While it was mandatory for all births to be recorded as of the day of birth in hospitals or private residences where a doctor or medical personnel were in attendance this was not always adhered to when friends and relatives delivered the child. The Municipal Archives and Records Center has stated that during those early years few of the births are recorded under the name of the child. Many were not named at the moment of delivery and the doctor was not required to obtain the name of the infant but only the parent's name, date of birth, sex and location of birth.

Almost all of the older births are therefore listed under the names of the parents or parent and rarely under the name of the infant. They are likewise cross-indexed in this manner. This is why Bonney's birth has been so elusive. Secondly, his birth was November 20th and not November 23rd.

Bonney never had a father named William H. Bonney, Sr. for this is the alias assumed or given him by March 1878. His father was named Edward McCarty and was not married to Bonney's mother. Edward also fathered brother Joe. Edward's identity was given in an article by a policeman who not only identified Edward as the father of the boys but also the date of Bonney's now-famous stabbing and the particulars surrounding the dastardly affair.[10]

Edward McCarty, no relation to Catherine, was a married man with a wife, a son and two daughters in Brooklyn. He was sometimes known as "Dad" McCarty. He kept a fruit stand at the corner of Nassau and John Streets and it was thought that he had some money. Henry's father did not die in 1862 for Edward McCarty lived until 1878 and a few months later his wife and son followed him in death. At the time of the interview in July of 1881 Officer Dwyer stated that both of Edward McCarty's daughters were alive and at that time still resided in Brooklyn.

Edward's name appears as the father on the birth record of a male child born to Edward and Catherine McCarty on November 20, 1859, at 70 Allen Street. No other McCarty child, save one, was born between 1857-1862 but to the wrong parents. This child had a sister and a younger brother. William Bonney had no sister and his brother Joseph M. McCarty was five years older.

According to the immigration listings from ships' manifests entering the Port of New York between 1846-1851 which may be found in **The Famine Immigrants, Lists of Irish Immigrants Arriving At the Port of New York 1846-1851** (volumes 1-3) only eight Catherine McCartys entered New York and only one was fated to become the mother of Billy the Kid.

One was only three years of age, one was 12 with five brothers and sisters, another was 22 with a husband and infant child, one 26 and married, three were too old and only one was born in the correct year of 1829. She is listed as Catherine McCarty, age 17 years, single, her occupation was that of a servant. She had arrived aboard the good ship **Devonshire** at the Port of New York on April 10, 1846, out of Liverpool, England. Original port of origin was Dublin. She came alone for no other McCarty was aboard the ship with her, having escaped the horrors of the Irish Potato Famine then raging in Ireland.

No birth certificate for young McCarty or his brother will ever be found for none exist. Birth certificates were not then requirements of law and few were requested and few issued. If one was requested, one or both parents would have to go to city hall and fill out the information sheet which also requested the legitimacy of the child. When this was completed a birth certificate was then issued and the recorded birth record revised to read under the child's name and not that of the parents. This was not done in the case of either son. Since only Catherine's name appears on the birth record of Joe and not that of the father it is a timely indication that it was out of wedlock. [11]

The **Sun** article gives us much information on young Henry, the child destined to become the most famous outlaw in American history. When news of his death reached New York City it was a generally-held belief in the Fourth Ward section that William H. Bonney was the former Michael (Henry) McCarty. Officer Dwyer of the Oak Street Station had known the young delinquent since he was a small child and was known around the ward by his first given name of Michael. He was well-known to the police of that precinct as a juvenile delinquent ever since childhood. [12]

Even today it is not uncommon for a person to be known by two different names. Sometimes a parent will call their child by one name while he is known to his friends by another. (A case in point is President John F. Kennedy who was known simply as Jack. Western killer Robert Allison was known as Clay Allison. Edmund (Edmond) Kiley of Silver City was known as Ed Moulton.)

The description of the two individuals and their personal appearance and coloring were identical down to the protruding two front teeth. Dwyer described young Michael as being a boy five feet five inches in height with blue eyes, brown hair and the upper two front teeth projecting outwards. Michael Henry McCarty and Henry McCarty/Antrim/William Bonney were identical in every detail.

The **Sun** reporter also interviewed twenty of Michael's former classmates and gang members, friends and comrades and all were in agreement that both men were one and the same person. They were not alone in their opinion.

A day prior to the **Sun** article, the **Dallas Weekly Herald** ran a front page article that stated that Billy the Kid had been killed at Fort Sumner and that he was a native of New York City. [13] Other newspapers printed similar statements across the country before the **Sun** article appeared. The **Las Vegas Daily Optic** stated, "A certain Mr. McCarthy, formerly of New York and better known as 'Billy the Kid'. . ." [14] People who knew him in Silver City and Lincoln all stated that he was from New York.

The following Saturday the **Optic** reprinted an article that had already appeared in the **Kansas City Journal** (no date given) which made the statement, "A New York policeman says the renowned 'Billy the Kid' was no other than little William McCarthy of the Fourth Ward, who, four or five years ago, when but seventeen years of age, committed one of the most unprovoked and atrocious murders known to the criminal records of that city."

One young man interviewed stated that he had been a former gang member with Michael McCarty and at the time of the interview was then working as a clerk in a grocery store located near Pearl and Hague Streets. He made the statement that the identity could be confirmed as Michael had been badly burned with acid on the upper part of his legs and body when around ten years of age. He had been taken to the Chambers Street Hospital and treated.

Although the city directories of that period do not list a Chambers Street Hospital there was indeed one located there. The month following the murder one Patrick Cully had died and his body was ordered to the Chambers Street Hospital on order of the coroner in order that an autopsy might be performed to determine cause of death. This appeared in an issue of the **New York Times**. [15]

According to Officer Dwyer, Catherine McCarty, Michael and Joe

16

departed New York in early 1873 as Michael had been "bound out" (foster home) to a western farmer. Since the journey would have taken over a month and a half and Catherine was married in Santa Fe on March first, Dwyer's schedule would be correct. Anyone entering New Mexico from back east would have to go down the Santa Fe Trail which ended in Burro Alley of that city.

Catherine Antrim's obituary stated that the Antrims had moved to Silver City only a year and a half previous to her demise. This would place their arrival in later April or early May of 1873. This would leave little time to have run a boarding house as one person claimed. Even J. Frank Dobie was misled by Upson for Dobie claimed Catherine ran a boarding house at Fort Union.[16] Fort Union was a military post and there were no boarding houses, civilian or otherwise. It is likewise doubtful that either boy had time to enter school in Santa Fe.

When Officer Dwyer made the statement that Bonney was "bound out" to a western farmer, he was entirely correct. There were five or six agencies in New York handling delinquent and orphaned children and **The Historical & Statistical Gazetteer of New York State 1860** and the archives verified this. When speaking of jails and juvenile delinquents it stated that, "Children are bound out at the age of 12 years." Further statements disclosed that these children were mostly bound out to other states and then only to farmers. Dwyer stated it was through the Children's Aid Society.

Under the heading of the Children's Aid Society it states that, "It has for its object to provide homes and employment for destitute children, and, to a limited extent, for adults of both sexes. Up to 1858 it had provided homes for 3,576. In 1857 it sent 468 boys, 200 girls, 28 men and 37 women to foster homes in other states." Even today, at the top of each page of their stationery, the words, "Adoption and Foster Home Division" appears. Michael McCarty was thus "bound out" to the foster home of a western farmer named William H. Antrim in New Mexico. The first time Catherine and William ever saw each other was when he met them in Santa Fe.

William H. Antrim was, at the time, 31 years of age and unmarried. He was not known to be good with the ladies and did not gamble, curse and rarely took a drink. He was looking for someone to wash his clothes, prepare his meals and take care of his home. Catherine was already dying of tuberculosis and a move to a drier climate was a medical necessity. She was also seeking someone to care for her children after she was gone. It was a mutually beneficial arrangement.

Officer Dwyer also stated that when Michael was about ten years old he was taken away by the Children's Aid Society and sent to the House of Refuge which ran industrial training schools. In one such school the child was allowed to attend school in the daytime and worked at the industrial school after hours and at night. Others were there full-time.

I contacted the House of Refuge for records but they said they did not maintain records on juveniles so I contacted the New York correctional system, the Supreme Court of New York and the Albany industrial school facility. According to all, New York did not maintain records on juveniles. [17] But they did in special cases.

A few days following the murder Michael committed in New York a 16 year old boy was brought before the Court of General Services for the crime of murder. He was sentenced to three years in prison and records were maintained on this individual.

In New York at that time there were several courts. There was the Supreme Court, Court of Common Pleas, Superior Court, Maritime Court and the Court of General Services. [18] All criminal cases were handled in the **Times** listing the disposition of all cases that appeared before them on that day. Though this boy was a year younger than McCarty he was tried in an adult court and the sentence entered into the docket book of that court. In New Mexico and other western states all cases were tried before the U.S. District Court or Justice of the Peace Court whether they were civil or criminal.

According to the court clerk in New York court records were only maintained if the individual was apprehended and tried for his crime. If the criminal escaped or was never captured, then no charge would be entered into the court records. Henry was never apprehended, therefore no indictment or charges were ever entered into the records against him.

Since Henry's father did not die until 1878, not in 1862 as Upson claimed, then who did die in 1862? A check of the death records for 1860-1864 disclose no Bonneys but there is one death listed for a McCarty. The man's name was William McCarty.

William McCarty, age 63 years, had been admitted to the Almshouse on March 25, 1862, in a destitute state. [19] Admission records disclose that he was a common laborer and his place of birth was Ireland. He had entered the United States through the Port of New York in 1849. He became seriously ill while in the Almshouse (Bellevue) and on August 11, 1862, was transferred to the Island Hospital where he died four days later. No cause of death was given. No death certificate has been found. [20] He was buried in a pauper's grave in the City Cemetery.

The records do not disclose marital status or next of kin. Upson was the only person to make the claim that Henry's father died in New York in 1862. Antrim said he understood that "Mr. McCarty died in New York" but that he could not verify this was true. Upson confused this with the early life of Dave Rudabaugh who did live in Kansas in the early 1860's. Though some have said his father was in the Civil War the Civil War Index records which list all participants in the military conflict on both sides does not list a single Rudabaugh name.[21]

Antrim's statement in this direction was preceded by the explanation that "It was not of his own knolage [sic]" was an admission that he was not certain that it was true. Antrim did not make the statement that this was Catherine's husband for it seems more than certain that in Silver City he was aware that his wife had never been married before. If this was an arranged marriage, then the Children's Aid Society would have certainly informed him of the facts surrounding his future wife and her children.

In order to determine whether Catherine McCarty might have divorced a husband in 1862, I checked the court records and discovered that this was false. No woman named Catherine McCarty had filed for divorce for several years prior to and following the year of 1862.[22]

To determine a possible relationship (father or grandfather) of William McCarty to Catherine, I contacted the President of the United States Lyndon B. Johnson and explained the situation. He ordered the Department of Immigration to check, and they telephoned explaining that they had such records on immigrants from the manifest of the ship they arrived on. If I could give them the name of the ship and date it had arrived in New York, they could give me information from the manifest. At that time this was unavailable. It was not until 1984 that I finally discovered this and obtained the information myself. A search is now being made for Catherine McCarty's naturalization papers in Washington, D.C. as well as in the New York court where she was naturalized.

I then contacted U.S. Senator Edwin Mechem and he brought my plight to the attention of the Consulate General of Ireland located at the Irish Embassy in San Francisco.[23]

The Consul General of Ireland, C.V. Whelan, suggested I contact Alf Mac Lochlainn, the Assistant Keeper of Manuscripts, at the National Library in Dublin, Ireland, for further information.[24]

According to Mr. Lochlainn's reply there was no nationwide survey of Ireland earlier than 1864 when civil registration of births and deaths was instigated. Prior to this there were but two sources available but neither was beneficial. The first source was the parochial registers located in the town where the individual resided but this is only of value if you know what that town is and whether Protestant or Catholic. You would also have to know with some degree of accuracy the exact area of residency.[25]

A national survey of householders was undertaken by county,

barony, parish and townland in 1850, but the names do not occur in any alphabetical order and the entire county would have to be scanned in order to locate any single individual. There was no indexing to this survey.

In 1850 in County Limerick alone there were some 300 or more McCarty households. McCarty is a common name in Ireland, particularly in the southern part and if the County Limerick total is reasonably accurate for all counties, then there could be at least 1,200 McCartys in S.W. Cork alone. The names Catherine and William are so common to the Irish that identification would be almost impossible.

A search of the 1860 and 1870 census reports for the Second, Third and Fourth Wards of Manhattan and the Third and Fourth Wards of Brooklyn have not yet disclosed a family unit composed of Catherine, Joe and Henry. There were numerous Catherine McCartys of all ages, including one of the correct age, scattered among families as domestics and unskilled workers but they are enumerated at the location of their jobs and not at their homes. There were many Henry and Michael and Joe McCartys but only one was below the age of 16 years.[26]

In the 1860 census for the New York Fourth Ward there was a three year old Michael McCarty alone in a building with his five year old sister. No adults were listed as being there as they were probably working, leaving the children to fend for themselves.[27] In January of 1873, an apartment house fire occurred and most of the victims were children left alone by their parents.

If Catherine McCarty were living alone as head of the household then she would appear so listed in one of the city directories but if she were living with her employers or with some other family, then she would not be listed. Only the head of the household is listed in city directories. Since the city directories sometimes do not list all people, it is possible she may have been overlooked. As an example is a listing of all Catherine McCartys from 1862 until 1870 as being the head of their household whether single, widowed or divorced.[28]

> 1862-1863 Three — one single.
> 1863-1864 One (a widow).
> 1864-1865 Five — one single.
> 1865-1866 Seven — one single.
> 1866-1867 Four — one single.
> 1867-1868 Eight — one single.
> 1868-1869 Nine — one single.
> 1869-1870 Four — one single.

Many of these women may be identified as widows for the name of their deceased husband appears alongside theirs but all constantly change addresses almost every year and sometimes do not appear in consecutive years. Could the single Catherine McCarty be Henry's mother?

From reading the death and crime statistics in New York circa the 1860's and 1870's it would not be difficult to understand the problems of living there and for wanting to get out. The great Potato Famine of Ireland sent thousands of immigrants flooding into America and the yearly statistics printed in a January 1873 issue of the **Times** disclose that each year Irish immigrants amounted to a minimum of 46% to a high of 56% of all immigrants into America. They came to escape starvation and during the Civil War there were many draft riots, some of the riots caused by the Irish themselves.

Being foreign citizens, many not yet naturalized in America, they were forced to register by the Union Army to fight in a war that was not their own. The **Times** related one case where Irish immigrants were working in a tobacco factory and were removed from their jobs in order to be conscripted for military service and replaced by southern Negroes who had fled the south. Many blacks were slain by the angry Irish.[29] The crime rate in New York was extremely high.

If the newspapers of that period are any indication of the degree of crime then New York City has certainly not improved. Crime was rampant. Many wards and districts were ethnically European and poverty abounded. Many of the wards had dirt streets that turned into lakes of mud when it rained and trash was often piled on the sidewalks. According to the Historical Society of New York, the east side Fourth Ward was a poverty area. Death, disease and hunger were very real to the inhabitants of those sections. The Fourth Ward fronted the east side docks where seafaring men of all nations docked daily, thus adding to the increasing burden of humanity.

Certainly the death rate for New York circa the 1860's was most appalling as testified by an 1869 issue of the **Times**. The article dealt with a comparison of deaths between the Fourth and Sixteenth Wards of Manhattan.

In 1867 the Fourth Ward where Henry McCarty lived registered 767 deaths plus another 187 by reason of infectious and contagious (zymotic) diseases. In 1869 that same ward recorded 691 deaths plus another 150 by disease. The Sixteenth Ward in 1867 had a combined total of 1,273 deaths by all means compared to 1,458 in 1869.[30] This was just two wards reporting out of twenty-two.

In the City of New York alone there were 22 separate wards and divisions with some sub-divided into as many as three smaller districts. Brooklyn had 19 wards and districts including Kings County and the City of Brooklyn.[31] Into such a life entered young Henry McCarty.

NOTES
CHAPTER 1

1. Municipal Archives & Records Center, New York City.
2. Ibid.
3. Ibid:
4. Birth records in Municipal Archives & Records Center.
5. **American Newspapers 1821-1936,** Bibliography Society of America. A search of all the above newspapers in New York. **New York Times Index, A Book of Records.**
6. **Roswell In Its Early Years,** by Maurice G. Fulton.
7. Upson letter to relatives dated December 25, 1878.
8. Ibid.
9. Ibid.
10. **New York Sun,** July 22, 1881.
11. Municipal Archives & Records Center, New York. Apparently his full name was Michael Henry McCarty. Partially verified by Chauncey O. Truesdell to Robert N. Mullin, Jan. 9, 1952, when he said that McCarty always used his middle name and never the first.
12. **New York Sun,** July 22, 1881.
13. **Dallas Weekly Herald,** July 21, 1881.
14. **Las Vegas Daily Optic,** July 28, 1881.
15. **New York Times,** Tuesday, Oct. 3, 1876.
16. **Vaquero of the Brush,** by J. Frank Dobie, p. 162.
17. Letters dated Feb. 1, 1965; Feb. 10, 1965; July 10, 1964; Feb. 4, 1965; July 17, 1964 and July 30, 1964.
18. Court column in all **New York Times** newspapers.
19. Almshouse records — Municipal Archives & Records Center.
20. Ibid.
21. **Official Records of the Union and Confederate Armies 1861-1865,** General Index.
22. Supreme Court, Court of Common Pleas, Superior Court, New York.
23. Telegram of Senator Mechem to author dated June 3, 1964.
24. Alf Mac Lochlainn letter to author dated June 15th and 24th, 1964.
25. Ibid.
26. 1860 & 1870 census reports for New York and Brooklyn.
27. 1860 census, Fourth Ward, New York. A Catherine McCarty of the correct age was located as a servant to a family but it is impossible to identify her as Henry and Joe's mother.
28. New York City directories 1862-1870.
29. **New York Times,** Tuesday, August 5, 1862, p. 8, col. 4.
30. **New York Times,** 1869. Date not written down.
31. Index to all New York and Brooklyn wards.

CHAPTER 2
THE STABBING

Ireland is composed mainly of two opposing religions: Catholic and Protestant. On the strength that the McCarty family might have been Presbyterian as the marriage occurred in a Presbyterian Church, I felt the possibility existed that they may have attended one of the Presbyterian Churches located with the boundaries of the Fourth Ward. Records might be maintained in the baptismal documents. There were nine Presbyterian Churches within this area during 1861-1872. They were mainly grouped in the area surrounding the streets of Pearl, Vandewater and Hague. [1]

Listed were the French Evangelical, German, German Mission, Grant Street, Mercer Street, Prince Street, Seventh, Spring Street, and West Church. [2] None of these churches and missions exist today.

All these churches were later transferred into the Presbytery of New York City. None of their records were maintained in New York but all records secured at the time of their dissolution were forwarded to the Presbyterian Historical Society in Philadelphia. [3] The records proved to be meager and incomplete and a brief search disclosed nothing of historical significance. A similar check was made of the local Catholic churches but was also fruitless. [4]

Little of young Henry McCarty's life in New York City is known but bits and pieces turn up from time to time. In the area he lived he most possibly would have attended the Vandewater Street School which later merged into the public school system of New York and became known as P.S. No. 1.

That Catherine McCarty remained in New York City until early 1873 is verified by policeman Dwyer, twenty close companions and records of New York City. All disprove that she ever saw Wichita. It proved to be another woman entirely.

According to one undocumented source, the Antrim family left Indiana in 1869 or 1870 and moved to Wichita. [5] The family Bible shows they moved to Newton, Kansas, where Levi died in 1879 and Mary Ann married. They were there until the early 1880's. James Madison spent some time outside Wichita with William and was still there in 1880.

Another claim was made that Catherine gained title to a vacant lot near Antrim's lot on September 12, 1870, and that Antrim gained title on March 25, 1870. The "lots" were 160 acre farm quarter sections owned by the government and known as Osage Trust Lands for homesteading and ultimate purchase. Both Antrim and Catherine homesteaded their land in the summer of 1870, filed for title in 1871 and received their title patents in May and December of 1873 after planting crops, trees, building a home, fences, corral, well and hedges. Antrim had the northeast quarter section while the Indianapolis Catherine the southwest quarter section. When Catherine gained title to her property on May 1, 1873, Antrim had been married to Bonney's mother for two months and living in Silver City. Antrim gained title in December of 1873 but did not actually receive title until February of 1874.

Antrim did make a supporting statement for the Indianapolis Catherine as law required ownership of federal lands only by citizens past the age of 21 years. "I have known Catherine McCarty for 6 years past; that she is a single woman over the age of twenty-one years, the head of a family consisting of two children and a citizen of the United States." James Madison Antrim gave the supporting statement for his brother.

Unfortunately this had led some to mistakenly believe that the Indianapolis Catherine McCarty and Bonney's mother were one and the same woman. They were not. In actuality they were two completely different women living in two different states as attested by the records. They simply shared the same, common Irish name but so did many other women. Had anyone bothered to check out the Indianapolis Catherine they could have settled the issue years ago.

It was a simple matter to go back in Indianapolis and census reports to locate this Catherine McCarty, her husband and her child. There were several Catherine McCartys in Indiana just as there were in Kansas and New York City. There were equally as many William Antrims.

In Indiana in 1850 there were two William Antrims and three in Kansas in 1850 and another in 1860. William H. Antrim may have been related to several other William Antrims. Ohio had two in 1850 and Pennsylvania also claimed two. Illinois had several and by 1860 and 1870 Ohio, Illinois and Indiana had even more. There were two outlaws named William McGinns, four William Wilsons, several William Bonneys, two Blackjacks, many Billy the Kids and innumerable plain Kid.

William Antrim's father, Levi, had a son named Levi C. and there were several other Levi Antrims in Ohio, Indiana and Kansas. In 1850 in New York the rolls show 19 unmarried Catherine McCartys and twice that amount of married ones. There were two Catherine McCartys in Madison County, Indiana, with William Antrim in the 1850 census. In 1870 not one could be located in Sedwick, Shawnee, Butler and Salian Counties in Kansas.[6] There were countless Mary, Thomas, James, John, Bridget and Ida Antrims. The list is endless.

In the states of Ohio, Indiana and Illinois the Antrim name is found in abundance. In Indiana alone in 1840 there were 17 Antrim families, four more with the spelling of Antrem and another two with the spelling of Antram. Three of the heads of households were named William Antrim.[7]

In 1892 Henry J. Cook, purchaser of the Catherine McCarty real estate in Wichita, made the statement that after selling him her property Catherine McCarty and her children moved to New Orleans six months later and to his knowledge remained there for some time.[8]

According to one article the Antrim family moved to Wichita in 1870. Actually the family was in Newton, Kansas, as shown by their family Bible records and William H. and James Madison were 2 miles outside Wichita city limits. Antrim's own statements place him in Kansas in 1869 or 1870 and he departed Kansas in 1872.

That he departed in the company of an old friend named Charles N. Munns is not yet verifiable but both are in the records as co-owners in several mining interests in Socorro County and Munns appeared as a witness for Antrim in several government pension applications. No Catherine McCarty has been proven to have left Kansas with him. One source claimed Antrim went to Globe, Arizona, although Antrim himself made the statement that he came directly to New Mexico. No Catherine McCarty appears in the Antrim family history until their wedding on March 1, 1873, in Santa Fe, New Mexico. Antrim relatives knew nothing of a Catherine McCarty prior to the brief marriage.

The 1870 Kansas census report discloses only one married woman with the name of Catherine McCarty, three adult male McCartys and one family named McCarty. Brother James Madison appears in Wichita with his new bride of a few months and was a saloon keeper.

Two Antrim families do appear, however, in the Shawnee and Saline Townships. One was in the town of Salina. This was Isac and Liddie Antrim with their children Clinton P., Levi J., Fanna, Elnora, William B., Ida D., Hattie P., Florina, Mary and the illegible name.[9] The remaining children were born in Illinois.

In the Township of Silverlake in Shawnee County was Eli and his wife Annie with their two daughters Mary A. and Nancy N. The parents were natives of Missouri and both girls had been born in Kansas.[10]

William Antrim's profession in Kansas was that of a farmer. It is significant that William and Catherine met and married in Santa Fe for it is here that the Santa Fe Trail from the east ends. All available evidence is that it was an arranged marriage as Antrim was to become the foster-father for young Henry according to New York law. Neither Catherine nor William had ever met until that moment. They stayed in Santa Fe approximately two months before making their home in Silver City which was to be Catherine's final resting place. Henry had arrived in the new land that would soon find him a niche in American western history.

Was it possible that Henry and Joe were enrolled in a school in Santa Fe during those two months? There were but three schools in Santa Fe at the time and only one was available to them. Two were Catholic. One was the San Miguel College and the other was the Roman Catholic convent Leoneviento de Nuestro Senorita La Luz. The final school was open to the general public and that was the small Presbyterian Church School known simply as the Presbyterian School and run by Reverend D.F. McFarland.

Reverend McFarland's school was small in comparison to the larger Catholic ones. It remained in operation until 1878 when it was finally absorbed into the Santa Fe Academy. [11]

An article appeared in an issue of the **New Mexico Magazine** which made the statement that Henry attended school there under his teacher Miss Charity Ann Gaston who had arrived in Santa Fe through the auspices of the Auburn, New York, Female Bible Society which had raised $500 for her transportation and first year's salary. According to the article Miss Gaston supposedly stated that she was unable to influence her undisciplined and unruly student Billy the Kid. However, the records of the school do not support such a statement for the names of Henry and Joseph McCarty do not appear on their list of student's names. Apparently they did not attend school during the two months they were there. [12]

An ironic thing occured about the time the Antrims were preparing to depart Santa Fe. A Mr. Lasker who was bookkeeper for the Spiegelberg Brothers Store was vacating his position to become the bookkeeper at the Sutler's store of Lawrence G. Murphy and James J. Dolan located at Fort Stanton in Lincoln County. He was being replaced by Morris Bernstein.

> Mr. Morris Bernstein, all the way from London, has taken Mr. Lasker's place as bookkeeper for Spiegelberg Bros. He is a lively pleasant, business like little gentleman and comes with the very best recommendations from large establishments in the Old World. We think that Mr. Bernstein will sustain his reputation and prove a valuable bookkeeper to the firm that has employed him. [13]

A few months later Bernstein would replace Lasker at the Murphy-Dolan establishment in Lincoln County. From there he would go to work for the Mescalero Apache Reservation where he would be killed in self-defense by Anatascio Martinez whom he was attacking. Henry was not present at the affray but later on writers would unjustly give him credit for the killing. Was it possble that the Antrim family might have visited the Spiegelberg Brothers Store before leaving Santa Fe and met Mr. Morris Bernstein?

Around the first of May 1873 the Antrims arrived in Silver City and moved into a rented, wooden frame home at the end of Main Street beside the Big Ditch that often overflowed during periods of moisture. Their home was next door to the **Enterprise** newspaper.

It will surprise many to discover that although Upson said the Antrims ran a boarding house in Silver City they did not. This contention has come about through a series of misinterpretations, confusion and assumption. The mistake is a logical but honest one.

No one living in Silver City at the time of Henry Antrim has ever made the statement that the Antrims owned a boarding house. A schoolmate of Henry's, Chauncey O. Truesdell, informed Robert N. Mullin in 1952 that he did not remember the Antrims running a boarding house. This opinion has been voiced many times by those early settlers who personally knew the Antrims. Everyone who made this statement came to or arrived in Silver City after Mrs. Antrim's death or up to seven years after Henry escaped jail and fled the town.

A.E. Lesnett told Robert Mullin that Edith L. Crawford of Carrizozo told him she came to Silver City in the spring of 1877. She stayed in Silver City at the hotel run by "Mrs. Antrim." (Of course, Catherine Antrim had been dead for almost three years at that time and Henry had been gone for two and was then living in New York). While Miss Crawford was there Mrs. Antrim told her of her young "son" and of how he had to leave the country so she fixed him up some clothes and a lunch, tied them in a red bandana and kissed him goodbye. She never heard from him after that.

Another interview in the Mullin file was from a woman who said that she arrived in Silver City in 1882 and stayed at a rooming house of a woman that told her about William H. Bonney and that this woman informed her that she had taken Henry in when his mother died and was his foster mother. The woman did not know the lady who ran the rooming house but later learned that the woman was William Bonney's mother — Mrs. Antrim. Catherine Antrim had been dead eight years at that time.*

The woman was neither Mrs. Antrim nor William Bonney's mother. She was Mrs. Brown who ran a boarding house and when Mrs. Antrim died she later took Henry in and he waited tables and washed dishes. Because Henry lived at the rooming house and Mrs. Brown was his foster mother some people have confused the issue and mistakenly

*Neither woman had ever seen or met Catherine Antrim and since Bonney lived with Sarah Brown in her boarding house they falsely assumed she was his real mother.

thought the woman was his real mother, Mrs. Antrim, though she was long dead.

A woman wrote me from Silver City and said she arrived in that town in 1882 and had known William Antrim well. She said she had seen the Antrim home many times over the years and described Mrs. Brown's boarding house. The Antrim home was two or three small rooms, much too small to take in boarders with four individuals already living there. The Robert N. Mullin photo that appeared in his book **The Boyhood of Billy the Kid** is not of Catherine Antrim but actually that of Mrs. Sarah Brown.

Other fallacies have cropped up over the years. An article by Maurice G. Fulton in the 1930 issue of **Folk Say** entitled, "Apocrypha of Billy the Kid" made two unbelievable statements. The first was that Henry was born in County Limerick, Ireland (Phil Rasch also claimed Levi Antrim was born in County Limerick when he was born in Ohio), and that his father's name was Williams. His two "sisters" were ravaged by the landlord and when Mr. Williams protested he was promptly thrown into jail where he soon expired. Catherine then took Henry and the two "sisters" to Nova Scotia where she married William Antrim and later came to New Mexico in 1869.

The second was that Henry stole a keg of butter and sold it to a Chinese man who reported him to the hotel owner where he worked. In revenge Henry stole the Chinese man's coat and was arrested. When he escaped he went to the cabin of the Oriental where he slit his throat while he slept.*

Even Governor Lew Wallace was not above making errors when it came to William Bonney. In his autobiography Wallace claimed that Henry came to Indiana when ten years of age and lived in Terre Haute and Indianapolis where he was raised and known as William Bonney. Another individual claimed Henry was called "Bonney" by his classmates in Silver City for some unknown reason but no one else ever heard of this incident.

The **New York World** issue of July 26, 1881, falsely claimed Henry was brought up in New Mexico as a child at a stage station (similar versions say a saloon and sometimes a store). His mother ran the station and later married a soldier in 1866. This came from Santa Fe attorney Charles H. Gildersleeve when he visited New York in July of 1881.

William A. Keleher, the noted New Mexico historian, once told Robert N. Mullin that Mrs. Adelaide Jaramillo, granddaughter of L.B. Maxwell, didn't believe that Henry had been born in New York. In 1938

*Over the years there have been a thousand folk tales (all untrue) surrounding Bonney but many writers have written these as facts without bothering to research the stories and what has been folklore and lies are constantly repeated as truths.

she claimed Henry had been born on a ranch near the Texas-New Mexico border and that his parents had been killed by Indians. Another version says his parents had been killed by Quantrill's guerillas during the Civil War.

Mary Ann Richards of England was the first schoolteacher in Silver City and apparently Henry's only teacher for she married in mid-1875 just before Henry escaped from jail and left Silver City forever. Since his death other people have claimed to have been his teacher. They were Miss Laura Gage (Mrs. Thomas Lyons), Charles Baylor, Dr. G.W. Bailey and Dr. J. Webster. One woman claimed to have taught him in Santa Fe while another claimed she taught him at Fort Union. There were no civilian schools or civilian schoolchildren at Fort Union.

The dry climate of New Mexico did not abate Catherine's tuberculosis and it progressed rapidly and at the end of the first year she was forced to take to her bed for the following six months. She never recovered from her illness and died on Wednesday, September 16, 1874, at the age of 45 years. The funeral was held the following day at the Antrim home at 2 p.m. [14] She was buried in section D-E27-14. September 16th was also the first day of school for Henry.

William Antrim knew so little about his wife that for the remainder of his life he would write her date of death as September 13th. [15]

In all honesty we do not know what Catherine McCarty Antrim looked like. The now famous photograph was first published by Eugene Cunningham but he could not authenticate it nor would he even divulge the source of the photo. He was requested to leave this information in his will for future history but he did not. No one in Silver City that knew her has ever verified this photo as being Catherine Antrim.

In 1969 Robert Mullin published a second photo purported to be that of Mrs. Antrim but it is Mrs. R.H. (Sarah A.) Brown, age 21 years at Mrs. Antrim's death according to the 1880 census. Catherine died at age 45 and the woman in the photograph is a much younger woman. Sarah Brown had the only boarding house in Silver City until 1879 and that closed not long afterwards. Mrs. Brown's boarding house was still in operation in the early 1880's. She and her husband were from Canada and they had a son, Robert H., born in 1874.

Little is known of Henry's life in Silver City and much of it is contradictory and confusing. Almost nothing is known of Catherine and Joe. Mr. Antrim was often out of work and sometimes worked as a laborer. He worked at the Ed Moulton sawmill in the mountains outside of Georgetown and once he supposedly worked in a butchershop run by Charles Bottom. To show how people confuse things in later years Betty Reich of District Number Four in Deming told Robert Mullin that it was

Henry who worked in the Bottom butchershop although Henry was too young and still in school at the time.

She also claimed that Henry was arrested for larceny at Mowry City (it was someone else) on the Old Butterfield Trail later known as Old Town. She also claimed Henry was arrested for breaking into a home and stealing shirts but broke out of jail with a man being held for an Arizona crime. Actually Henry did not do the stealing and he escaped alone.

The Antrim home is another source of dispute and constant contradiction. Citizens who arrived in Silver City after Mrs. Antrim's death constantly confuse the Brown boarding house for the smaller, more simple Antrim home. Mullin's photograph shows a man in twentieth century clothing in front of the home (the Antrim home washed away in 1895) and nestled against the foothills. The Antrim home at the end of Central Street and the Big Ditch does not have hills near it for several hundred yards in any direction.

Catherine was only able to get around for six months before she became bedridden and then never left the house so few people even knew her. No one seems to remember anything about her other than she was a "jolly woman." No physical description of her has even been given by those that knew her. Brother Joe fared no better. All that was remembered about him was that he was bigger and older than Henry and sat in the back of the schoolroom. Most people do not even remember him. Both are apparent non-entities in American history.

While William and Joe apparently got along without difficulty this was not the case with Henry. He had spent fourteen years of his life in the undisciplined streets of the Fourth Ward and was a gang member of a group of street toughs. Suddenly he found his world shattered. Now he had to answer to, and pay for, his erring ways. He could not and would not accept fatherly domination. Despite published stories by uniformed writers there is no proof that his father ever abused Henry. People who knew him state quite the opposite was true. Antrim always treated his family kindly and with respect but he could not get along with Henry because the boy would not mind him (to a certain degree) and Antrim could not put up with Henry's stealing. Henry was the only problem in the Antrim household.

William Antrim was a quiet, personable man who was beloved by all who knew him and had such a friendly outgoing manner that he was called Uncle Billy. He did not drink much, never engaged in brawls and disliked rude jokes and behavior, though his father Levi was known as a man that liked his toddy and was often inebriated. [16]

Antrim's memories of his famous stepson were somewhat different than those of former Silver City classmates who enjoyed their moment in the sun when they gave their versions some 75 years later. Antrim stated that he remembered Henry as a cruel, little sneak thief who stole everything he could get his hands on. [17] This pattern, set early in his life, formed the basis for his behavior in later years. Henry was born to be bad and there was nothing that Mr. Antrim could do about it and it frustrated him.

Sarah Ann Knight had a younger brother named Anthony B. Conner who was a former schoolmate of Henry's. Though all young boys are possessed of the spirit of mischief at times, what is bad behavior to one person is totally acceptable to another. Conner stated that in his personal opinion Henry Antrim was probably a much better boy than he had been. This, of course, is a natural reaction. [18]

Sheriff Harvey Whitehill, the first man known to have arrested Henry in New Mexico, had a son named Harry who said that he didn't think that Henry Antrim was such a bad boy after all. [19] Sheriff Whitehill did not share his son's opinion. He disliked Henry because he was a sneak thief. Henry's teacher, Miss Mary Richards, felt that her student was probably no worse than any of the other boys and that he was an average student who helped out with the chores around the little schoolhouse. Her opinion was probably colored by the fact that she liked Henry and that Henry admired her because he and his mother were both ambidexterous as was Mary Richards. Because of this Henry told her he felt they must be related. [20]

When William Antrim gave Henry a brand new Barlow pocketknife as a present Henry rewarded him by beheading the neighbor's kitten with it. [21] Henry's inner-self was already beginning to appear at the surface and although outwardly he appeared to be an average boy he had volcanic churnings inside his heart that were leading him to destruction.

Sometime during the year of 1875 Sheriff Whitehill apprehended Henry Antrim for the first time. A rancher identified only as Webb had some butter in his buckboard and left it unattended for a few moments. Henry spied the butter and realized the monetary value that such a commodity would bring on the open market so he removed it and sold the butter to the merchants around town. When Webb reported the butter missing it was not difficult to trace it to the culprit. Soon Henry was in the clutches of the law. The only thing that was done to Henry on this occasion was that Whitehill, who stood 6 feet 2 inches tall and weighed 240 pounds, liberally applied the palm of his large hand to the Antrim **gluteus maximus** in several brisk movements.

It is clear from an interview years later that Whitehill did not like Henry Antrim. [22] Whitehill clearly stated his distrust of Henry because

31

Henry had, as he put it, a peculiar facial characteristic common to all outlaws alike. His eyes were never at rest, always shifting, always roving, ever on the move.

Henry's second offense was of a more serious nature. George Shaefer stole some clothing and/or possessions from two Chinese named Charlie Sun and Sam Chung. He hid his booty and when he desired a shirt he sent Henry Antrim to retrieve it for him, which Henry did. The goods were valued at $70.00. Henry was given some of the clothing for helping Shaefer which he stored in his trunk at Mrs. Brown's boarding house. Mrs. Brown soon discovered it and reported it to Sheriff Whitehill who promptly arrested Henry while George Shaefer made himself scarce.

Henry was tried, convicted and sentenced before Justice of the Peace Isaac Givens to a short term in jail. A search of the old J.P. records and the **Register of Prisoners** book disclosed that prisoners who came before the J.P. court did not go before the grand jury nor await their indictment. The J.P. had a wide power of office at that early time.

At the time, according to the 1880 census report, Isaac Givens was 35 years of age and single. A native of Tennessee as were both his parents, he was normally a miner by profession as was William Antrim.[23] We do not know the length of time young Henry was incarcerated but being a juvenile and a first offense he certainly would not have been in jail for a long period of time, particularly as an accessory. The notice of his "capture" and subsequent escape was duly noted in the local newspaper.

Henry McCarty, who was arrested on Thursday and committed to jail to await the action of the grand jury, upon the charge of stealing clothes from Charlie Sun and Sam Chung, celestials sans cue, sans joss sticks, escaped from prison yesterday through the chimney. It is believed that Henry was simply the tool of "Sombrero Jack" who done the actual stealing whilst Henry done the hiding. Jack has skipped out.[24]

Charlie Sun, a single, male Chinese, worked in Silver City doing washing and ironing. He was 25 years of age at the time of the theft.[25]

Henry did not like the embarrassment of being arrested nor the close confinement of a jail cell and did not intend to remain long. His escape was not an individual effort but planned and aided by outside companions. According to some statements which may be found in the Robert N. Mullin file in Midland, Texas, a half-Mexican/half-Anglo named Manuel Taylor who had a mining claim at nearby Chloride Flat, was the principal in the matter along with several of Henry's close companions.

Due to the age of Manuel Taylor and the fact that he had to ride in from Chloride Flat leads to the conclusion that "Sombrero Jack" might have made the arrangements. It is more than certain that Henry had known of the escapade for it was he who requested to Sheriff Whitehill to be left in the outer room unguarded. Whitehill did so and left after locking the front door from the outside. Many have claimed Whitehill knew of the rescue and allowed Henry to escape since he was not the culprit but only a tool of the thief. However, the sheriff's prisoner book discloses that they had full time jailers at the time and jailers never left the jail unguarded when prisoners were there.

Supposedly Taylor climbed on top of the roof of the jail. Chauncey Truesdell claimed the jail was made of wood slats laid atop each other while others state it was of adobe. Taylor, aware that Henry was alone in the outer room that contained a fireplace and no flue, lowered a rope at the proper time. This occurred, according to one version, when Whitehill and Deputy A.H. Moorehead went to eat and left the jail unguarded (where was the jailer?) in the meantime. The actions of two lawmen leaving a jail unguarded while prisoners were still inside is a bit on the fanciful side. Jails were never left unguarded when prisoners were there which was most of the time according to Whitehill's jailer's book.

To add further to an already flimsy tale, another individual claimed that the jail door had no lock or hinges so the two lawmen simply propped a mesquite branch against the door and went to dinner! However, the jail had both hinges and locks and mesquite is not native to the Silver City area. There would be no reason to climb up a chimney if the branch was removed from the door. Of such folklore are legends made.*

We do not know what might have become of Henry Antrim had he stayed and served out his short sentence. In all probability, judging from all the evidence presented, it would not have made any difference at all for he would have become what he had always wanted to be.

Contrary to the **Enterprise** remark that Henry was awaiting action of the Grand Jury, he was not. Anyone sentenced and tried by a Justice of the Peace was never indicted by a Grand Jury.[26] If this were true then under Territorial laws of New Mexico an indictment would have been issued and entered into the Criminal Docket Book whether the person was at large or in custody or whether the individual's name was even known. This was not done in Henry's case for he had received all the legal formalities required under Justice of the Peace offices. Whether the defendant is physically present or absent is not a requirement under New Mexico law in district court but it is under the Justice of the Peace courts. Persons were charged under a first or last name only, a

*Whitehill stated that he locked the door from the outside and records show that a contractor built the jail. All other doors in town had locks and hinges so why wouldn't the most important structure in town?

nickname or no name at all. In such cases two blank dashes are left beside the charge and are what we today call "John Doe" charges.

Henry's whereabouts the next few days are unknown but he was hiding around Silver City or Georgetown. At least five different people have claimed Henry came to their house and they smuggled him out of town. According to the Chauncey Truesdell version, Henry came directly to their home, was given some clothes and sent to stay with a Mrs. Dyer until they could decide what to do with him. The following morning they then made him a nice lunch and put him on the stage bound for Globe, Arizona.[27] This same version was claimed by his foster mother Sarah Brown and a woman named Mrs. T.W. Holson. Mrs. Sarah Knight and Mary Richards Knight said Henry came directly to their ranch after walking 15 miles on foot through Apache infested territory. Robert Black stated that Henry came to him and he made Henry wash the soot off his clothes and body and he gave him some boy's clothes to wear in place of his soiled ones. Black also claimed to have given Henry a note to take to Whitehill stating that he would be responsible for Henry. Henry never took the note to Whitehill for he went directly to the only person that could possibly help him — William H. Antrim in Georgetown. Antrim was working for Henry's other friend Ed Moulton.

It was ironic that Robert Black had been the contractor that had built the jail that Henry had escaped from.

Miss Mary Richards Casey had quit teaching school in 1875 to marry rancher Daniel Casey. She was 25 years of age at the time and later had five children. They were Edith, Simon, Blance E., John E. and Patience. Patience later became Mrs. Patience Glennon and told her mother's story to **The Southwesterner** in 1963. Her mother had told her that Henry had walked the dangerous 15 miles to their ranch and informed them of what had occurred. They put him in the barn for a few days while they decided what course of action to follow.[28]

Henry requested a horse and some money but they countered with his returning to Silver City and giving himself up. He agreed and a horse was loaned him. Although they saw him years later they never saw the horse again. The problem with all of these versions is that some of the people are talking about two different instances two years apart and they were unaware of his presence during the two year lapse. All assumed that he was in Arizona. He was not in Arizona the first year after escaping from Silver City.

Several works concerning the life of Henry McCarty Antrim in Silver City have been based solely on the Upson version and recollections of Chauncey O. Truesdell. Chauncey had stated that he was born in 1864 in Michigan which would have made him 11 years of age at the time of

Henry's escape. The 1880 census report contradicts his age twice. On June 1, 1880, Chauncey Truesdell appears in the census report for Georgetown staying in the home of George W. Holt and family. Chauncey often went to Georgetown approximately 20 miles distant. Chauncey himself gave his age to the enumerator as 12 making the year of his birth 1868. He said he was a son living at home and had attended school that year.[29]

Four days later, on June 5th, a different enumerator appeared at the Truesdell home and the following information was given by his parents.[30] Chauncey's father was G.J. Truesdell and his mother was named Callie. Chauncey had one brother named Gideon and a younger sister named Julia. The Truesdell's gave Chauncey's age as 14 making the year of his birth 1866.[31] This would mean that Chauncey was only 7 years of age when the Antrims arrived in Silver City and only 9 years of age when Henry escaped. Henry was 16 at the time and it is hardly believable that a 16 year old boy would consider a 9 year old boy as one of his friends.

It is evident from the 1950 Truesdell letter to descendants of the Ed Moulton family and the 1952 interview with Robert N. Mullin that Chauncey's memory was highly influenced and colored by what he had read and heard over the 75 year period since he had last seen Henry McCarty Antrim.

Chauncey stated that his family placed Henry on the stagecoach to Globe where Henry later engaged in a card game with a Chinese man whom Henry caught stealing. The Chinese drew a pistol first but Henry shot him and escaped. This is actually a mixture of three separate stories and two different men. The Chinese gambler was Charlie Sun of Silver City. This was substituted for the Irishman, Frank P. Cahill, who was not even armed when shot and we do not know the circumstances of the dispute and killing. Thirdly, it was brother Joe who was supposed to have gone to Globe, Arizona, not Henry. Actually, following the escape Henry and Joe were returned to their old haunts in New York City, presumably by William H. Antrim.

Confusion as to who Henry went to see after escaping could certainly come from the fact that perhaps he may have gone to the homes of several people seeking help but ending up with the one person who not only would help him but had enough money to get him out of the territory. To send a 16 year old boy with a lunch and two or three dollars in his pockets to the distant city of Globe with no prospect of a job and no financial means to support himself while seeking employment and no place to stay does not sound plausible. Henry needed a lot of money fast and someone old enough to make the arrangements to remove him from the territory and the only person that fit these standards was William H. Antrim.

A short while later Henry and Joe reappeared in the Fourth Ward section of New York City a year prior to Henry's stabbing a young man to death there. Henry re-entered the familiar world of the streets that he knew so well. It was here, a year later, that he committed the now-famous stabbing so adulterated by Ash Upson in his folklore.

Upson's version is a composite of true facts, wrong dates, wrong places and wrong people. It must be remembered that Upson was not writing a historical biography of William Bonney but simply a swiftly (but poorly) written bit of folklore designed to make Pat Garrett and himself a quick bit of money they both needed so badly. According to the Upson version a blacksmith insulted Catherine Antrim in Henry's presence and the angry Henry threw a rock at the older man. Another version says he did this to Charlie Sun and this is why he was arrested.

A few days later, in a saloon, Ed Moulton got into a fight with several men, one of whom just happened to be the blacksmith in question. Henry saw his chance, leaped upon the blacksmith's back, clinging to him with both arms and legs, and somehow miraculously reached into his pocket to get his pocketknife, opened the blade (how?) and stabbed the blacksmith to death. No such incident ever occurred in Silver City. The actual killing was somewhat more bizarre and ghastly. Henry was two and half months short of his seventeenth birthday at the time, not twelve as claimed by Upson.

Ed Moulton has always been the central figure of this saga and in his own words he said it wasn't so. Some writers claim it was Moulton's saloon while others say it belonged to another man. The Moulton family records and history, as well as the real estate records for Grant County, disclose that Ed Moulton never owned a saloon in Grant County, although he might have worked in one in 1874 for a short period of time. [32] Mr. Moulton was a well-known personality around Silver City and Georgetown and always denied the story given by Upson.

Sheriff Whitehill also denied the story along with the man who supposedly owned the saloon and the entire population of Silver City along with the Silver City **Enterprise** and **Grant County Herald** newspapers. However, Ed Moulton did tell his family exactly what did occur.

A blacksmith had insulted Catherine Antrim's reputation but it is unknown whether it was in her presence or not. Henry was present at the insult and took immediate offense to the remark. He pulled out his pocketknife which the bigger and stronger man easily took away from him and the man began slapping Henry around. Ed Moulton chanced to see the uneven affray and stepped in and knocked the blacksmith down.

The incident ended there. There was no stabbing although a few rumors claimed he did cut the blacksmith but Upson's book angered many citizens when it was printed.

At age twelve Henry was still in New York City associated with The Children's Aid Society and the police of the Oak Street Station in the Fourth Ward and did not leave New York until "bound out" by them at age thirteen according to New York State laws. Henry made no attempts to hide the stabbing. In fact, he seems to have made certain that everyone he came in contact with knew of it to enhance his reputation as a "bad man." There is no evidence that Upson was ever in Silver City and no one there remembers him but he did know, by word of mouth, that such an incident had taken place and assumed that it had occurred in Silver City.

While Ed Moulton was a distinguished and well-known man in Grant County he certainly was no man to fool with physically. He also had his own problems with the law in Grant County. He had a charge of larceny against him and his employee, William H. Antrim, appeared as one of the jurors in his trial. [33] In the civil records there was a divorce case pending against him and his wife Sarah and one filed for adultery. [34]

Ed Moulton owned a sawmill on the Mimbres River near Georgetown somewhere in the vicinity of the Anthony Ranch. When William Antrim was out of work and in need of employment Ed Moulton hired him to work at the mill.

William Antrim succeeded in getting his stepsons out of the Territory and back to New York where they were known. By removing Henry out of the Territory he would be safe for there were no extradition rights in those days and a crime in one state was not held liable as a crime in another. Only now Henry and Joe had to support themselves financially. It is not known whether their father, Edward, assisted them during this period but he certainly did immediately following the stabbing.,

In 1881 Policeman Dwyer gave a history of Henry's life in the Fourth Ward as Dwyer had known him since childhood and said he had been a delinquent always in trouble and well-known to the police at the nearby Oak Street Station. He gave information as to Henry's being "bound out" as a delinquent child in early 1873 to a farmer out west and of his two year absence before returning to the Fourth Ward along with his brother Joe. He stated that Henry returned to the Vandewater Street School he had once attended and he also became an apprentice tinsmith. We do not know Joe's profession but he had been out of school for several years and had worked in Georgetown.

This was the same, familiar neighborhood that he had been raised in and according to his friends and the police he quickly took up his old ways and former comrades. He belonged to a group of boys known as "half-grown men" who frequented the streets stealing, fighting, drinking and raising general disturbances. Henry also was known to get intoxicated at times. [34]

There were three major newspapers in New York at that time and all described the murder. One ran it under the title of "Murder on Vandewater Street," another entitled it the "Pearl Street Murder" and the third refered to it as the "Fourth Ward Murder." [45]

The murder occured on a Saturday night, September 9, 1876. Henry had been back in New York for a year. Henry, Joe and a young companion named Thomas Moore and two unidentified girls had been drinking heavily and ended up in front of the Matthew Dwire store and saloon located at 369 Pearl Street near Hague. The local toughs had made Dwire's store their official hangout, according to the news reports, and purchased much of their liquor from Dwire as there were no laws regulating drinking ages then. It hadn't taken Henry long to get back into the fast pace of New York after two dull years in New Mexico. There was no William H. Antrim to tell him what to do.

One of the boys that belonged to this new gang was named Thomas Moore, age 20, an Irish immigrant. Moore lived only four doors away from Henry at Number 5 Vandewater Street while Henry and Joe occupied Number 9. Moore worked in a brush factory on Fulton Street and was the sole support of his mother. Until this moment Moore and Henry had been on good terms and there was no bad blood between them. That is, until that night.

Henry was just two months short of his seventeenth birthday when the small group paused in front of the Dwire store shortly before 11 p.m. on a Saturday night. The group became engaged in conversation, according to witnesses, and then Moore made a remark to Henry that angered him and an argument quickly ensued which then turned into a fist fight. Apparently Henry was getting the worst of it for he suddenly broke free and dashed into the Dwire store where he secured an empty beer mug in one hand and a 12-inch cheese slicing knife in the other and returned to the street.

Henry threw the beer mug at Moore and Moore easily dodged it, but then Henry pressed close and raised the huge knife. Moore saw the knife coming and raised his right hand in a defensive posture in a vain effort to ward off the impending blow. The knife passed between the thumb and first finger of the right hand, slashing it to the bone and severing an artery in passing. Officer Dwyer said it looked as if the thumb had been almost cut off.

The tip of the blade then penetrated the left cheekbone to the bone just below the left eye and split open the cheek as the blade drove downwards and buried itself to the hilt at the base of the neck just above the sternum and collar bones. This was a fatal wound that severed a major artery. Henry withdrew the knife and quickly fled the scene in haste leaving behind brother Joe and the two girls.

Moore did not die immediately but staggered down the street where he collapsed into the arms of a friend in front of 357 Pearl Street. The boy laid Moore upon the ground and summoned the police from the Oak Street Station. Moore was now unconscious. Moments later Officer Dwyer and his fellow officers arrived upon the scene where bystanders lifted Moore's body in their arms and carried him the two blocks to the stationhouse where he was laid upon the floor. Moore slowly bled to death.

Joe and the two girls were taken into custody on the spot and removed to the Oak Street Stationhouse where they remained all night.

The Oak Street Station was a precinct house located at numbers 9 and 11 Oak Street. In the late 1880's it became the Fourth Precinct and later changed to the Fifth Precinct during the 1900's. The exact date of the change is not presently known.[36]

The officers in command at the time of the Moore murder were Captain Robert G. Webb, Sergeants Richard F. Magan, Peter Ryan and John Kelly. Captain Alexander Williams was assigned to the Moore murder and he was in charge of the investigation.

No Officer Thomas Dwyer was found on the meager records left to the city but records disclosed one John Dwyer was appointed a policeman in that precinct on May 25, 1863. This would coincide with Dwyer's statement that he had known Henry most of his life. Dwyer also worked in the Eighth Precinct and was noted for his "great energy and vigilance which he displayed in arresting no less than nine murderers."[37]

The police were able to trace Henry's flight down Hague Street then through a passageway to 84 Frankfort Street where he threw away the knife which was recovered. Henry was followed all the way into Brooklyn where his father Edward lived where the police lost his trail.[38]

Joe and the girls remained behind in the Oak Street Station where Moore lay bloody and lifeless on the dirty floor. The only communication the stations had between them at the time was a telegraph system which they used to notify all stations to be on the lookout for Moore's murderer. Afterwards they telegraphed for a doctor.

Joe and the girls were released the following morning on the orders of the coroner. Neither the police nor the newspapers ever released the remark Moore made to Henry that caused him to commit murder. It was days before the police discovered what happened to Henry and Joe.

Upon his release Joe made his way back to his father Edward in Brooklyn where he joined Henry who had arrived the night before. The three suddenly disappeared from sight and rumors among the Irish were that Edward had taken the boys back to Ireland although this was impossible to do overnight due to government red tape, passports and other regulations. Edward remained gone for approximately three months before he returned and everyone learned that he had returned the boys to their stepfather in New Mexico. During their absence Captain Williams issued a statement to the press that he was certain of securing the young murderer's arrest. [45]

THE FOURTH WARD MURDER

The body of the youth Thomas Moore, who was stabbed and killed by a companion named Michael McCarty, now at large, on Saturday night at Hague and Pearl Streets, was removed from the Oak Street Station yesterday morning to the residence of his parents at No. 5 Vandewater street. Disfigured by three horrible wounds, the body presented a ghastly spectacle as it lay in the small miserably-furnished apartment, surrounded by a group of wailing women and girls, near relatives of the murdered young man. Coroner Croker arrived at the house at 12:30 a.m. accompanied by his deputy Dr. Mac-Whinnie, who cleared the room, and made the usual postmortem examination. Tracing the course of the wound in the neck, he found the weapon used by the murderer — a twelve inch cheese knife — entered immediately above the sternum or breast bone, severed the jugular vein, and passing under the right clavicle, penetrated the apex of the right lung. The wound in the face extended from the left cheek to the maxillary bone; and the gash on the right hand, which was probably inflicted as the victim endeavored to ward off the thrusts of his assailant cut the radial artery between the index finger and thumb.

The direct cause of death was hemmorage. At the conclusion of the autopsy the mother of Moore, in answer to the usual questions, stated that her son was twenty years of age, a native of Limerick, Ireland, from which place he, in the company of the other members of the family, immigrated to New York thirteen years ago. The efforts of Captain Williams and his officers to effect the arrest of McCarty; and to learn to circumstances of the quarrel, that lead to the killing Moore, was, up to a late hour last night, unsuccessful. James McCarty, a brother of the murderer and two women, who were detained at the station house as witnesses, were discharged on an order from the coroner. [40]

40

In order to gain a better perspective of the killing and view the usual inaccurate and contradictory newspaper information that makes the historian's job harder, a second version is given here for benefit of the reader.

A FOURTH WARD MURDER

TWO COMPANIONS QUARREL AND ONE STABS

AND KILLS THE OTHER.

Thomas Moore, aged nineteen, a brush maker, who resided at No. 5 Vandewater Street, was stabbed in the throat and almost instantly killed by Michael McCarty, aged twenty, a tinsmith of No. 9 Vandewater Street, at a late hour last night, during a fight at the corner of Pearl and Hague streets.

Moore and McCarty had been friends and associates, and as far as can be ascertained, no previous quarrel had occured between them. They belong to a group youths and half-grown men who make their headquarters in front of the grocery and liquor store of Matthew Dwire, no. 369 Pearl Street. They had been drinking together during the evening, and it is stated that they were both under the influence of liquor. Shortly before 11 o'clock they were standing with some friends in front of the grocery referred to when a dispute arose between them. The cause of the quarrel was not ascertained, as those who were present during the dispute were reticent about the affair. The disputants soon resorted to blows, and a scuffle followed, during which McCarty drew a large bladed pocket knife, and made a lunge at his antagonist. The point of the blade struck downward, the blade imbedded itself in his throat, inflicting a ghastly wound from which the blood poured copiously. The wounded man sank to the pavement and McCarty fled and in the confusion and excitement which ensued succeeded in making his escape. Moore was picked up by some of the bystanders and carried to the Oak Street Station, scarcely two blocks away, and was laid on the floor of the sitting room. A surgeon was telegraphed for, but in less than ten minutes after he was brought to the station Moore expired. McCarty is well known to the Police of the Fourth Precinct, and Capt. Williams is confident of securing his arrest. A general alarm was sent over the Police telegraph to every stationhouse in the City, warning the Police to be on the lookout for him. The body of the murdered man is at the stationhouse awaiting the action of a Coroner.[41]

The final version is from the Sunday, September 10, 1876, issue of **The Sun.**

MURDER IN VANDEWATER STREET

Thomas Moore, of 9 Vandewater Street, was killed last evening by

Thomas McCarthy, at Pearl and Hague streets. Moore was about 20 years of age, had worked in a brush factory at Fulton Street, was the only support of his mother, and would have finished his apprenticship in October next. After quitting work last evening he went home and gave his mother his week's wages and started out soon after with McCarthy's brother, who was soon after parted with him. Moore as was his custom went to Matthew Dwyer's grocery at Franklin and Pearl streets. Moore was not liked much in the neighborhood on account of his prowess and jealousy existed between him and other young men.

Moore stepped to the sidewalk outside Dwyer's store, and, meeting Thomas McCarthy, a quarrel arose between them. Thomas McCarthy rushed into the store, snatched a large meat knife from the counter, ran back to the sidewalk and plunged it into the throat of Moore, who sank to the pavement. McCarthy then ran down Hague Street, and through a passage to 84 Frankfort Street, where he threw away the knife, which Capt. Williams soon after found, and which Dwyer identified as the one taken from his counter. Moore lived but a few moments after he reached the Oak Street Station. On examination, it was found that the lower carotid artery had been severed, and his left thumb cut off.

Thomas McCarthy is eighteen years of age, and works sometimes in a tin factory in South Street. He had not been arrested.

The offical inquest did not appear in the papers until several weeks following.

THE PEARL STREET HOMICIDE

The inquest in the case of Thomas Moore, who was stabbed and killed by a companion named McCarthy, at the corner of Pearl and Hague streets, on the night of September 9, was held by Coroner Weltman yesterday. Several persons were examined, and it was clearly shown that McCarthy had stabbed the deceased. Mr. MacWhinnie gave it as his opinion that Moore had died from hemmorage caused by stab wounds, and the jury concurred in the belief that the latter was inflicted by McCarty. The murderer escaped in the night on which he committed the deed and has not since been arrested. [42]

The formal indictment charges against Michael Henry McCarty have never been found and never will be for there are none. According to the Municipal Archives & Records Center they do maintain the records of the court of General Sessions but only in cases where trials were held and verdicts rendered. Since McCarty was never apprehended there would be no records. Unlike most court systems New York City had five separate ones. They were the State Supreme Court, Court of Common

Pleas, Superior Court, Maritime Court and the Court of General Services.[43]

According to the daily law column in the **Times** only one court handled criminal cases and that was the Court of General Services. The **Times** reported that the Grand Jury would meet two weeks following the Moore murder and continued well into early October. Grand Jury indictments were never printed and cannot be found unless they came before the court for trial.

In 1876 the Court of General Services was normally handled by Mr. Gildersleeve the Recorder unless the case load was extra heavy. In such cases they held two courts and the name of the accused always appeared in the **Times** along with the crime he was charged with and the outcome.

The law column proves that it is untrue that juveniles did not have records maintained for that very section disclosed several individuals, age 16, that were bound over to the prison system. One was a sixteen-year old boy who had committed a murder and was sentenced to three years in the state prison for adults. Where the defendant was in custody there was an indictment and trial records were maintained.[44]

NOTES
CHAPTER 2

1. Municipal Archives & Records Center letter of July 10, 1964.
2. Presbytery of New York City letter of Oct.5, 1964. Presbyterian Historical Society letter of July 23, 1964.
3. Ibid.
4. Chancery Office, Archbisopric of New York letter of May 4, 1965.
5. **Westerner's Brand Book, Los Angeles Corral, 1956.** "A Man Called Antrim," by Phil Rasch.
6. 1810, 1820, 1830, 1840, 1850, 1860 and 1870 census reports for above counties and states plus real estate, probate, will and tax records. The Indianapolis Catherine McCarty and her husband Dennis and son arrived in the U.S. between February-May of 1860.
7. 1840 census report for the State of Indiana.
8. Henry J. Cook statement of July 8, 1892.
9. 1870 census, Township of Salina, Kansas, June 29, 1870.
10. 1870 census, Township of Silverlake. July 29, 1870.
11. Presbyterian Historical Society records of the McFarland school.
12. **New Mexico Magazine,** "The First Presbyterians' First Hundred Years," May 1967.
13. **Santa Fe New Mexican,** Tuesday, April 29, 1873.
14. **Silver City Enterprise** obituary. September 18, 1874.
15. Throughout his life Antrim would never remember the month & year of his marriage or the church it was performed in.
16. **Historical Sketches and Reminscences of Madison County, Indiana,** by John L. Forkner and Byron H. Dyson. Published in 1897.
17. **The Westerner's Brand Book; Los Angeles Corral, 1956.** "A Man Called Antrim," by Phil Rasch.
18. **The Boyhood of Billy the Kid,** by Robert N. Mullin. pp. 11-12.
19. Ibid.
20. **The Southwesterner,** June 1963 interview with Mrs. Patience Glennon, daughter of Miss Mary Richards Casey.
21. **The Westerner's Brand Book; Los Angeles Corral, 1956,** "A Man Called Antrim," by Phil Rasch.
22. **Silver City Enterprise** interview of January 3, 1902.
23. 1880 census, Silver City, Grant County. June of 1880.
24. **Grant County Herald,** Sunday, September 26, 1875.
25. Silver City, Grant County census report, June 7, 1880. p. 22, line 45.
26. Grant County Criminal Docket Books, J.P. Records and the Register of Prisoner's Book.
27. Letter of Chauncey Truesdell dated Sept. 29, 1950 (his first version).
28. **The Southwesterner,** June 1963.
29. 1880 census, Georgetown, Grant County, NM. June 1, 1880.

30. 1880 census, Silver City, Grant County, NM. June 5, 1880.
31. Ibid. Also the Robert Mullin interview of Jan. 9, 1952, which Chauncey gives contradictory information from his earlier letter.
32. Records of the Ed Moulton family and Grant County Real Estate Records supplied by Sandra Crittenden, wife of the grandson of Ed Moulton.
33. Moulton family letter to author dated April 5, 1984. Grant County Criminal & Civil Docket Books 1875-1883.
34. **New York Sun,** July 22, 1881, interview with Officer Dwyer and 20 of Henry's friends and companions.
35. **New York Times,** Sunday, Sept. 10, 1876, Vol. XXV, No. 7797, p. 1.
   The World, Sunday, Sept. 10, 1876, Vol. XVII, No. 5500, p. 1.
   The Sun, Sunday, Sept. 10, 1876, Vol. XLIII, No. 363, p. 1.
36. Letter of Detective Thomas Krant, Historian & Museum curator of the New York City Police Department. Letter dated 1984.
37. Ibid.
38. **New York Times,** Sunday, September 10, 1878.
39. New York Times, Sept. 10, 1876, Vol. XXV, No. 7797, p. 1.
40. **New York Times,** Monday, Sept. 11, 1876, Vol. XXV, No. 7798, p. 8.
41. **New York Times,** Sunday, Sept. 10, 1876, Vol. XXV, No. 7798.
42. **New York Times,** Sept. 29, 1876, col. 5, p. 5.
43. Law columns appearing daily in the **Times,** Municipal Archives letter dated July 22, 1984, from Kenneth R. Cobb.
44. A search was made in the records of the Court of General Sessions and Supreme Court from February 7, 1876, to December 19, 1884, and no records on McCarty were located. The court clerk stated that records were only kept in cases where the defendant came to actual trial. In McCarty's case he did not do so therefore no records were maintained but I believe that an indictment was issued and is still in existence.

CHAPTER 3
THE CAHILL KILLING

Edward McCarty must have been surprised to see his two sons and even more surprised to discover that one of them was a murderer. Edward took them by train or wagon to where the Santa Fe Trail began at St. Joseph, Missouri, and evidently rode with them down the long, dusty road that led back to New Mexico and Henry's final destiny.

It is now apparent that Officer Dwyer's statement concerning the financial condition of Edward McCarty was correct for he had to pay the fare for three to Santa Fe and one in return. To Dwyer's credit it must now be stated that everything he said about Henry in July of 1881 has since proven to be correct in every detail down to the time tables. Not a single mistake could be found.

Whether Edward took them by stage from Santa Fe to Georgetown is uncertain. It is equally possible William Antrim went to Santa Fe and picked the boys up himself. Though both boys left Silver City at the same time in 1875 only Joe was in evidence after their return for Henry proceeded to Camp Grant, Arizona. Joe remained around Georgetown for several years at various jobs, possibly working for Ed Moulton at his sawmill. Henry (then Bonney) made occasional visits to see brother Joe from time to time and friends placed him there until at least the early part of 1880 for he does not appear in the June census for that year. By that time William Antrim had likewise departed and was living in Mogollon where he remained for the next 33 years. Local citizens assumed later that Henry had spent this two year period in Arizona from 1875-1877 when he murdered Frank P. Cahill at Camp Grant. They hadn't known he had been back in New York.

Little is known about Joe other than he departed Grant County in early 1880 and did not reappear again until he met Pat Garrett in a restaurant in Old Town Plaza in Albuquerque to discuss the details of the death of his brother at Fort Sumner. In 1883 he appeared in the Albuquerque City Directory working as a clerk for a hotel, then disappeared completely from history until emerging in Denver, Colorado, some 30 years later.

Henry was still wanted for the theft of $70.00 plus the escape from the Silver City jail therefore he could not remain in the county or the Territory for long. It would seem certain that he departed Georgetown soon after his return and it may have been this instance that oldtimers were speaking of when they assisted him in getting out of town for their stories were told more than 50 years after the occurrence. The earliest he could have departed from Arizona would have been in the latter part of October or early November at the latest. No one in Grant County saw him from the time of his jailbreak in 1875 until his occasional visits back to Georgetown in 1878 to 1880. By then his reputation was well known over the Territory from the Lincoln County War and his career as a petty rustler.

The Truesdell and Richard versions concerning Henry were not given until many long years afterwards. Truesdell's was 74 years later and was greatly influenced by the Cahill murder as well as the countless books and articles which both had read during the intervening years. They only related what they could recall from memory and time dims all trails. Neither was aware of the New York episode so it is easy to determine how their memories had come to accept that Henry had been in Arizona all the time. One event blended into that of another and Henry often replaced others in various incidents.

Henry arrived in southeastern Arizona and would have immediately sought employment. He would work the following ten months for his own keep. There would be no one to lean on or to give assistance. There are as many conflicting stories concerning where he worked as there are fingers on your hands. Many of the oldtimers of that area all knew a young man who worked at the same ranch as they did and although they didn't know his name they were all "certain that it had to be Henry Antrim." One claimed Henry worked with him while another swears it was at another location. One man said Antrim worked as a freighter for the military at Camp Grant, stole some mules, was apprehended and jailed but later escaped. Military records prove this was another individual and not Antrim. There is no absolute evidence that will verify where or for whom he was employed or the length of time. Freighters had to be experienced and Henry had never freighted. The most easily attainable job available to him was that of a cowhand. From later documentation it appears Henry had also learned the art of gambling and perhaps taken up the sideline of being a part-time pimp.

This ten month period of his life is an absolute blank. In Arizona he was just another drifting young man coming from nowhere and heading for nowhere. He was no different from anyone else in southeastern Arizona and blended into the crowd. He was simply known as Henry Antrim and government documents show that sometime during this period someone had dubbed him with the nickname of Kid. At seventeen he looked and acted much younger than his years. Such persons were always dubbed Kid.

Southeastern Arizona was a battleground dominated by the wily Apache. It was a violent land filled with violent people. Camp Grant was located 35 miles north of Tucson at the junction of the Aravaypa and San Pedro Creeks. It was desolate country with water flowing only in the rainy season. Officers often enjoyed bathing in the clear pools of trapped water in the rocks just below their quarters where the creek came out of the sand. Armed guards were posted along the rocks above the pools where the officers bathed in order ward off Apache attacks. On more than one occasion Indians attacked and killed the defenseless bathers.[1]

The Apache were so bold they often killed openly at the front gate in full view of the guards. Bourke related one incident where an Apache warrior covered his body with mud, tied clumps of grass to his head and crawled to within 75 yards of the front gate where he then lay in wait. Presently an unsuspecting soldier rode out and when he was within striking distance the warrior jumped out from his place of concealment and lanced the hapless soldier to death while the guards looked on helplessly. By the time an armed body of troopers reached the spot the Apache had disappeared. It was into such a violent atmosphere that young Henry Antrim now found himself. He was a boy in a world of men.

Camp Grant was a rectangle composed of officer's row, adjutant's office, post bakery, guard house, commissary storehouse, quartermaster's storehouse, enlisted men's quarters, sutler's store and all arranged in the shape of a square. A little distance behind the quartermaster and commissary warehouses was a blacksmith's forge where the calvary horses were kept in fine shape.

One of the blacksmiths here during the early 1870's with the 5th Cavalry was a man named John "Windy" Cahill whom some writers have mistakenly felt was the man Henry killed.* Next to the forge was the butcher's corral and the cavalry stables. Behind this was the San Pedro where the Army horses were broken to the saddle in a loose, sandy spot. Nearby were prehistoric Indian ruins where bored soldiers passed the time away digging up artifacts.

There were three types of living accomodations available at Camp Grant. One was built of adobe and originally intended for use as an Army kitchen in 1857. Many Apache style **jacal** huts were in evidence, being constructed of upright logs chinked with mud and roofed with a mixture of mud and branches. Canvas was stretched over the inside of the roofs in order to catch the falling centipedes and scorpions. The final type of quarters was the standard military issue canvas tent.

*The evidence is presented in this chapter that they were two different men and that blacksmith Cahill was no longer at Camp Grant at that time. The post returns do not mention the murder nor Cahill. The returns also show the post employed a civilian blacksmith. Henry Runte was the blacksmith in March of 1877 and in September of that year it was T. Sullivan.

Only two types of recreation were available to the bored, frontier soldiers. Gambling was by far the most popular and it was ten cents to come in and maintained by a twenty-five cent limit. The second choice was fighting red and black ants by placing them together in a jar and betting on the outcome. Off post in nearby civilian saloons they pursued drinking, whoring, fighting and gambling.

The man Antrim murdered was named Frank P. Cahill. The legend later grew that this was the same blacksmith named John "Windy" Cahill spoken of by Lt. Bourke in his book **On The Border With Crook.** Bourke and Cahill were attached to the 5th Cavalry at Camp Grant. Bourke mentions Cahill as being a member of the infamous expedition north to the Salt River Cave (Skeleton Cave) where the 5th Cavalry slaughtered a mixed band of Apaches, their women and their children. The soldiers fired into the roof of the sloping cave, causing the bullets to ricochet into the huddled Indians in the rear of the overhanging slope.

One warrior managed to slip out of the cave in an effort to contact nearby Apaches for assistance and made it to the rim of the canyon where he paused momentarily to shout his defiance at the soldiers below. John Cahill is supposed to have killed him with a long shot. Thus Bourke stated that John Cahill's name should be inscribed in Arizona history. [2]

On August 17, 1877, Henry Antrim shot Frank P. Cahill in cold blood in the stomach and then fled the country for New Mexico. Cahill was unarmed and unprepared for what occurred and died the following day. A Tucson paper recorded Cahill's deathbed statement of the incident.

Frank P. Cahill was shot by Henry Antrim alias Kid at Camp Grant on the 17th, and died on the 18th. The following are the dying words of the deceased:

I, Frank P. Cahill, being convinced that I am about to die, do make the following as my final statement: My name is Frank P. Cahill. I was born in the county and town of Galway, Ireland: Yesterday, Aug. 17th, 1877, I had some trouble with Henry Antrem, otherwise known as Kid, during which he shot me. I had called him a pimp, and he called me a s____ of a b____, we then took hold of each other: I did not hit him, I think: saw him go for his pistol, and tried to get hold of it, but could not and he shot me in the belly. I have a sister named Margaret Flannigan living at East Cambridge, Mass., and another named Kate Conden, living in San Francisco. [3]

A second article in a Tucson paper added a little more information to the affair and disposed some myths concerning Frank Cahill.

Austin Antrim shot F.P. Cahill near Camp Grant on the 17th instant, and the latter died on the 18th. Cahill made a statement before death to the effect that he had some trouble with Antrim during which the shooting was done. Bad names were applied each to the other. Deceased had a sister — Margaret Flanegan in Cambridge, Mass., and another — Kate Conlon in San Francisco. He was born in Galway, Ireland, and was aged about 32. The coroner's jury found the the shooting "was criminal and unjustifiable, and that 'Henry Antrim alias Kid' is guilty thereof." The inquest was held by M.L. Wood, J.P., and the jurors were M. McDowell, Geo. Teague, T. McCleary, B.E. Norton, Jas. L. Hunt and D.H. Smith.[4]

These two articles tell us several things. One is that Henry Antrim was clearly identified as the murderer and that Cahill was unarmed and shot down in cold blood. Since the Coroner's Jury was composed of a civilian Justice of the Peace and six other civilians Cahill was a civilian and not a soldier, for military personnel inquests are held by the military and presided over by officers.

The article of the 23rd is also the first documentation of the use of the alias of Kid by Henry Antrim. This contradicts an earlier statement by one writer that James McDaniels gave Henry the sobriquet of Kid later that fall in Mesilla. It also tells us that Cahill was not a Negro, as previously thought, nor was he a military blacksmith.

Both the above articles have been known to historians for over twenty years but I offer in print a third and more conclusive document which discloses that Antrim was not the same young man who stole the mules nor was Antrim jailed for the murder.

The government has, and continues to be, the greatest record keeping organization in the world, the military not excluded. Anything occuring on military property or concerning the military would be listed in the records of that post. These records are in the Retired Military Records of the General Services Administration in Washington, D.C. In order to determine whether the two Cahills were one and the same man or different persons I checked the Retired Military Records for Camp Grant reposing in Washington, D.C. In order to locate any soldier at any given time all you need is to present the soldier's name, post, the date he was there and, if possible, his unit. A search was made between 1872-1877 and the Retired Records Division stated that there was no John Cahill or Lt. Bourke there during these years, therefore the two men are not one and the same though they share the same last name.*

The military telegrams book for Camp Grant did mention the murder as well as the theft of mules which occurred at the same time. The

*The 1870 census report for Camp Grant shows Lt. Bourke still there but no one named Cahill. The only Cahills in Arizona were a Francis at Camp Crittenden and Martin at Rio Verde. Neither man appears in the 1864 census.

telegram was directed to the U.S. Deputy Marshall W.J. Osborn in Tucson from the Commanding Officer of Camp Grant Major C.E. Compton and dated August 23, 1877.[5]

TELEGRAM

GRANT A.T.
August 23, 1877

Osborn W.J.
    U.S. Deputy Marshall
        Tucson
594   Cahill was not killed on the military Reservation
L.R. 704 His Murderer, Antrim, alias "Kid", was allowed
        to escape and I believe is still at large.
Of the mule thieves we have apprehended the soldier and
        will try him by Court Martial.
His accomplices have not yet been arrested.

C.E. Compton
Major, Comdg

Major Compton substantiated the news articles that Henry Antrim alias Kid was indeed the culprit and that the murder did not occur on military property. Henry was not prevented from fleeing the scene therefore he had not escaped jail. This telegram and the **Arizona Weekly Star** issue of August 23, 1877, is the earliest documentation of the use of the alias of Kid.

A further check was made of the records for a possible inquest report on Cahill as well as any federal charges against Antrim but there are neither. This is further verification that Cahill was a civilian. If the affair concerned a military man then there would be no need for Compton to notify Osborn of military affairs and problems. Since Antrim and Cahill were clearly civilian matters Compton merely made a courteous gesture in giving Osborn all the facts he had on the matter.

It is interesting to note that somewhere along the way Antrim had finally acquired a pistol which now made him as big as any other man. Cahill's accusation that Antrim was a pimp conjures up visions that Antrim had already made an alliance with a prostitute and was either cohabitating with her or perhaps receiving money from her.

A concentrated search for the crimnal docket books of that county was undertaken to locate the murder indictment (if any) against Henry Antrim but so far has not turned up. Arizona records in the Archives Branch, Federal Archives and Records Center in Laguna Niguel, California, were also searched without success. The inquest papers of the Justice of the Peace courts were thrown away long ago.

A further study of the Post Returns for Camp Grant disclose that the only civilians working for Camp Grant were a blacksmith, wagon mechanics and laundresses. The story that Bonney was captured and jailed at Camp Grant (which was impossible since it was a civilian affair and not a military one) is destroyed by the Post Returns which do not show Henry Antrim either being apprehended or jailed as lists of confinements and prisoners in the guardhouse are given monthly.

The soldier Major Charles E. Compton spoke of in the telegram was either John Foley or Zoel LeBel, for he placed both men in confinement that August to await trial by court martial. Foley was later transferred to Camp Lowell and LeBel to Camp Huachuca. There were no casualties shown for military personnel at Camp Grant not only for that August but for months preceeding and following the August murder.

Further untrue stories have cropped up from time to time confusing Henry Antrim with other men. In 1933 Anton Mazzanovich wrote an article for the **Tombstone Epitaph** issue of March 9, 1933, stating that Colonel Gilbert C. Smith of the Quartermaster Corps at Camp Grant stated that Antrim worked as a teamster for the post and stole a wagon and some mules along with some saddles but the Compton telegram repudiates this story along with the monthly post returns which show that no teamsters were employed by that camp.[6] There were 35 civilian employees most of whom were laundresses and wagon mechanics. Compton had already captured the mule thieves except one. All were soldiers of that post.

Mazzanovich also claimed that "the constable" complained to Camp Grant of Antrim's stealing government horses and mules but he could not effect arrest. Civilian authorities do not complain to the military authorities of civilian thefts nor vice versa. Had anyone stolen government horses and mules it would have become the business only of Major Compton, not the civilian "constable," and the military would have effected arrest. If Antrim was employed by Camp Grant how could an arrest not have been effected since he would be working at the post each day? Also, Antrim had no experience as a teamster which required more skill than becoming a cowhand. The military did not hire untrained personnel.

Judge Miles Leslie Wood, the Justice of the Peace who held the inquest over the body of Frank P. Cahill, was said to have arrested Antrim over the incident according to another source. The story went that Antrim went to the hotel (actually it was an eating house) located at Camp Grant (it was and remains against federal law for civilian enterprises to operate on government property. Why would a civilian hotel be needed on a military post that already provided housing for its personnel and had no civilian visitors?)

If you are able to accept the fantasy that Henry Antrim murdered an unarmed man and then went directly to the hotel of the local Justice of the Peace and rented a room that a $20 a month cowpoke could not afford, and waited to be arrested then you may just as easily swallow the remaining portion of the story. That, for some still unexplained reason, Wood prepared a breakfast tray for Antrim, laid a pistol under the napkin and served the murderer breakfast in bed! Upon which Wood, apparently ignoring that all civilian arrests were the responsibility of the local peace officers, pulled a pistol and placed "Antrim" under arrest and lodged him in the military guardhouse at Camp Grant where he later threw salt into the eyes of his military guard and escaped.

By law Antrim, being a civilian, could not be placed in a military stockade nor could Wood do so for it was for military personnel only. Wood had no authority to effect an arrest and no authority to place anyone in a military guardhouse. All persons arrested and/or placed in the guardhouse appear in the post returns records and those records do not show the name of Antrim or of any other civilian from March until November of 1877. When Major Compton wired Osborn in Tucson that Antrim had escaped it meant that he was not apprehended nor deterred from fleeing the scene. Later editions of the **Grant County Herald** disclosed that the remainder of the mule thieves were captured. Compton already had one mule thief — a soldier — in the guardhouse.

Henry Antrim was not a noted desperado in 1877. He was nothing more than snotty-nosed eighteen year old boy that hardly anyone knew or remembered until long after he became famous. Suddenly everyone in Arizona and New Mexico was a former friend of his. Thus they began recanting countless fairy tales about some young cowboy whose name they did not know but that they were "certain" was Billy the Kid. They mixed up the exploits of one individual with that of another. None of these individuals could even describe the fellow they knew and none ever knew his name but all were sure that it had to be Antrim. A lot of sudden, and longed for, attention was to be gained by these lonely and forgotten old men who, after 60 or 70 years, had sudden bursts of clear memory.

NOTES
CHAPTER 3

1. Lt. John G. Bourke's original military field reports in bound form in the University of New Mexico Coronado Room.
2. **On The Border With Crook,** by Lt. John G. Bourke and his field reports of that expedition. The military blacksmith's name was John Frank Cahill, not Frank P. Cahill. See p. 192 of Bourke's book.
3. **Arizona Weekly Star,** August 23, 1877, p. 3, col. 1.
4. **Arizona (Weekly) Citizen,** August 25, 1877, p. 3, col. 1.
5. Compton telegram of Aug. 23, 1877, from Retired Military Records & Archives Center, General Services Administration, Washington, D.C.
6. Smith was not a colonel at that time but a captain. Had he been a colonel he would have been commanding officer instead of Major Compton. G.C. Smith's son, Colonel C.C. Smith, reputiated this version in his letter to the **Tombstone Epitaph** in a letter dated March 30, 1933.

CHAPTER 4
MESILLA AND LINCOLN

After murdering Cahill, Henry "Kid" Antrim left Arizona rather hurriedly and one step ahead of the law. He was fast becoming an expert in the art of escaping retribution. He returned briefly to Georgetown and announced he was going to Lincoln County soon but his first stop was Mesilla.

Mesilla was a hotbed of criminal activity and rustling, the announced king of which was John W. Kinney. Kinney was born in 1853 in Massachusetts as were both his parents. Kinney had married a local Hispanic girl named Juana. The marriage was childless as of 1880.[1]

John Kinney was head of what was perhaps the largest cattle and horse rustling operation in New Mexico. Together with Jesse Evans, James McDaniels, Frank Baker, Sam Perry, James Whittacer (Whittaker), Tom Hill and others they plundered the southern part of the Territory robbing, rustling and murdering when necessary. Kinney owned a ranch outside of Mesilla where he kept stolen cattle with his own until he could dispose of them. In March of 1879 he opened a butchershop.[2]

Allegations toward the Kinney operation occasionally appeared in newsprint. A Mr. Samora reported his cow stolen and it was traced to a butchershop in Mesilla.[3] Charles Coleman had 14 head of cattle taken from him at the San Diego crossing on a Friday and they were also traced to Mesilla.[4] A Mrs. Toddhunter who lived five miles above Mesilla lost 15 head of cattle. Somehow John Kinney "found" them mixed in with his own herd and gracefully turned them over to the deputy sheriff.[5]

When Kinney opened his butchershop it gave him the opportunity to butcher and sell stolen beef rather quickly without having to run them out of the country to other locations. In the census report Kinney listed his occupation as that of a cattle dealer.[6]

Jesse Evans and company rustled cattle all over southern New Mexico and west Texas. Occasionally they raided into Mexico. They often disposed of their gains in Arizona and old Mexico. When times were slow they occasionally turned to robbing stores. These men were already established, hardened criminals long before Henry Antrim rode upon the scene and joined them in late August. It was at the knee of these men that the eighteen-year old lad learned his trade.

In Dona Ana County alone John Kinney had 22 charges filed against him for murder, assault to commit murder, killing cattle, buying stolen cattle and stealing cattle.[7] He had but a minor part in the coming

Lincoln County War where he was charged in the burning of the Alexander McSween home.[8] He had a solitary charge in the El Paso docket books.[9]

Jesse R. Evans had ten charges in Dona Ana consisting of murder, horse stealing and larceny of horses and mules. There were five in Lincoln for larceny, murder, horse stealing and accessory to murder while Pecos County, Texas, had two against him for Assault With Intent to Murder (Harry Ryan on August 3, 1979).[10] He was fined $5.00 for trying to kill Ryan and found not guilty on the other.

James McDaniels had seven charges in Dona Ana for murder, larceny and stealing horses plus one civil charge of replevin.[11] No charges appeared for Baker, Hill, Perry or Whittacer.

In January of 1880 James McDaniels was reported to be in jail in Chihuahua, Mexico, charged with "appropriating to himself horses and mules belonging to J.H. Riley."[12] He returned the following month and hearing the allegations printed concerning him he denied ever having been in jail in Mexico.[13] The following year, in January, he was in jail in Mesilla for the theft of horses from a Mr. Jerrel.[14]

It must not have taken Henry Antrim long to make their acquaintance and become a member, for less than two months following the Cahill murder young Antrim was duly reported in print for the first time in connection with a criminal element.

GRANT COUNTY ITEMS

On Monday last, three horses belonging respectively to Col. Ledbetter, John Swishelm and ____ Mendoza, were stolen from Pass coal camp in the Burro Mountains. On learning the facts Col. Ledbetter and Swishelm went out to the camp and trailed them in on the road at Apache Tahoe. Sometime on Tuesday, the party of thieves, among whom was Henry Antrim, were met at Cook's canon by Mr. Carpenter. Telegrams have been sent to Sheriff Barela at Mesilla, and we hope to hear of the Arrest of the the thieves and the recovery of the horses.

The thieves who stole the horses from the Burro Mountains last Monday, stopped the western bound coach 7 miles east of Fort Cummings, asked the driver if he "had anything on," and on his replying no, said, "Well, we'll let you pass this time:" insisted on Morehead taking a drink with them and finally rode off after remarking that they were leaving the country. There were nine of them each armed with two revolvers and a Winchester rifle, and carrying two belts with cartridges.

They fired at Geo. Williams at Warm Spring Ranche, but as George very promptly returned their fire, they left without unnecessary delay.

This gang is constantly on the road, and it is time that the citizens turned out and strung them up. [15]

This is the only written documentation that ties the name of Henry Antrim to the Mesilla gang. Henry was an apprentice learning his trade but he did not remain long for no charges were ever lodged against him in the entire southwestern part of the Territory for this theft and other crimes. The Burro Mountains are southwest of Silver City and although named openly as one of the guilty parties in the theft not one of the guilty parties was ever charged with the crime.

This article disproves the contention that Henry went directly from Arizona into Lincoln County. Though his sojourn was brief in Mesilla it did serve to further his apprenticeship in the company of hardened, professional criminals. His very presence in Mesilla at this particular time also discredits another story about him.

This version states that around the first of October in 1877 a hungry, footsore young man staggered up to the Heiskell Jones ranch near Seven Rivers and introduced himself as William Bonney. [16]

Not long after Mesilla, Henry Antrim did visit the Heiskell Jones ranch upon many occasions just as he did countless other ones across two states. However, he could not have been in Seven Rivers around the first of October if he was still riding with the Kinney bunch in Mesilla until late in October. It is also certain that he did not introduce himself as William H. Bonney for until March of 1878 he was still known as Henry Antrim and Henry McCarty in Lincoln County. He could not have arrived there for at least two or three months after this given date.

As near as can be ascertained he departed Mesilla in the latter part of October bound for Lincoln. Apparently the Mesilla bunch also temporarily broke up at this time for Jesse Evans, McDaniels and company also went to Lincoln where Jesse had the misfortune to get arrested. Charges against the group in Dona Ana County cease at this time.

Henry made a brief stop in Lincoln town where Sheriff William Brady hired Henry for a short period of time in the fall to help him harvest his crops before he moved on. When speaking of the future outlaw during this time period Brady never called him by the alias of William Bonney but always referred to him as Henry Antrim. This information was discovered by New Mexico State Historian Don Lavash, head of the New Mexico State Archives and Records Center from the Brady family.

There is also circumstantial evidence that while in Lincoln Henry helped break Jesse Evans out of jail. From here he proceeded into the town of Fort Sumner where he chanced to run into, and become friends with, Pat Garrett fresh from the Texas plains and recently retired from the trade of hunting buffalo. Many writers have attempted to claim that Henry and Garrett never met until Lincoln but this is untrue. Henry's best friend in the Lincoln County War was George Coe and he stated that both men were the best of friends before either came to Lincoln town. Sue McSween, wife of Alexander McSween also stated the same thing as have many others who were close to him.

Pioneer families of Fort Sumner were quite aware of this fact and the two men enjoyed playing casino together and gained the nicknames of Little Casino and Big Casino. Because of his tremendous height (6 feet 5 inches) Garrett was also called **Juan Largo** by the local Mexicans. They were an unlikely pair even in height and age differences but were often seen about Fort Sumner in the presence of each other. Because of his previous familiarity with the outlaw, Pat Garrett was hired by the Panhandle Cattleman's Association in Mobeetie in 1880 to capture, or kill, his former friend.

Fort Sumner had originally been established as a Military Reservation by Executive Order on May 28, 1869. On March 25, 1871, the Secretary of War relinquished the reservation to the Department of the Interior for disposition under the Act of February 24, 1871, (16 Stat. 430). The lands were surveyed, appraised and offered at public sale on January 15, 1884. The purchasers of this land were Eldridge B. Sopris, Lonny Horn, Sam Doss, Dan L. Taylor and Luther D. Hoggins.[17] However, the military had long abandoned the post and it was a civilian domicile long before the final sale.

The wealthy Lucien B. Maxwell moved his operations into Fort Sumner and when Mr. Maxwell died the management was passed to his son, Pete. The census report for 1880 shows Mrs. B. Luz Maxwell as head of the family at age 48 years. She was a naturalized citizen of New Mexico though her father was a Canadian married to a New Mexico woman. Pete was then 32 years of age and he had two sisters. One was lovely little Paulita who was 13 when she met Henry Antrim. Odilia was a mere 7 in 1880. Deluvina was the Navajo servant girl employed by the Maxwells and she was 19 when Henry arrived in Fort Sumner seeking his fortune. Deluvina was unable to read or write.[18]

At first Pete Maxwell liked the personable young man but in later years when Henry had acquired the reputation of a criminal his feelings changed. Pete disliked his sister associating with a known killer and it was a well-known fact around Fort Sumner that Paulita was one of Henry's paramours. Pete wanted Henry out of her life but he could do nothing about it. He said later that while he wanted Henry out of Paulita's life he was sorry it had to happen in the manner in which it finally occured. [19]

Henry worked for the Maxwells for a brief period of time and apparently no one was aware of his embryo criminal background. In a few short months he would be bragging about his exploits in order to establish his reputation as a man not to be trifled with.

It is a popularly held feeling among many historians that Pete Maxwell, whether directly or indirectly, was mainly responsible for Pat Garrett learning of Bonney's whereabouts that hot night in July of 1881. Word had reached Garrett by mail that the Kid indeed was not only in the Fort Sumner area but that he was staying in one of the Maxwell employee buildings. It certainly was no secret that Bonney had been staying in the Maxwell cow and sheep camps since his escape and that Maxwell must certainly have been aware of this fact. When Garrett arrived late that night it was to the room of one man and one man only that he went — Pete Maxwell.

George Coe gave proof of the Garrett-Bonney relationship in pre-Lincoln County many times. [20] Coe said the two attended **bailes** together and drank in the small saloons. Bonney felt safe in Fort Sumner, a fact not unknown to Garrett and others, and this weakness eventually led to his tragic death.

Henry did not remain in Fort Sumner long for he soon drifted south down the Pecos where he worked for a brief period for John Chisum. This has always been speculation but there is documentation to attest to this fact. A cowboy named William Henry Graham worked for the nearby John Slaughter ranch when he met Henry. Mr. Graham told his family he and Henry were friends in the early part of 1878 while Henry was a Chisum employee.

William Henry Graham was born in Coryell County, Texas, on August 12, 1862. He was a large man, weighing over 200 pounds and had left home at the age of fourteen to follow the herds. His first job was on the ranch of Mr. Forier in the Big Bend country. He later worked for John Slaughter and met Henry probably in January of 1878 and maintained relations with him for the next 2½ years. When Bonney was killed at Fort Sumner Graham rode down to find out the facts concerning the death of his friend. [21]

It is still uncertain whether Henry entered the town of Lincoln directly from Chisum's or whether he drifted down to Seven Rivers and drove a herd of animals stolen from a rancher by Jesse Evans. Whether he came with Evans or not is not known but what is known is this early connection with Jesse Evans in Lincoln. These cattle were sold directly to Lawrence Murphy and James J. Dolan who then disposed of them in their usual manner.

If Henry was working for John Chisum he was working for a particularly difficult man. Chisum was a wealthy man several times over but he was a man who rarely paid his debts or taxes (Pat Garrett was similarly inclined) and constantly filed charges of Replevin and Assumpsit in the Civil Docket Books in order to gain the property of many other individuals.

John Chisum registered two brands for his cattle. One was the ▬▬ and the other was the ⊥. It only took a few, quick turns of a hot running iron for Murphy and Dolan to turn this brand into their own registered brands of ◄◄ and ▭. To better facilitate the exchange of stolen cattle from Chisum herds between them and their friends David M. Easton and the powerful politician Thomas B. Catron of Santa Fe they were allowed to register the Murphy-Dolan brands on April 8, 1879.[22] In this manner stolen Chisum cattle could be branded with the Murphy-Dolan brand exchanged between all parties concerned without having the bother of making up a bill of sale for they could not be traced.

Once he was in Lincoln County Henry Antrim discovered that he was still among old comrades from Mesilla and everyone dealt with Murphy and Dolan, so it wasn't surprising that Henry should immediately take up with his old friends before going to work for John Tunstall. Even his new associates were no better than his former ones.

Charlie Bowdre was wanted for Murder and Assault Upon A House while Tom O'Folliard and Samuel Smith were both indicted on murder charges on April 28, 1879. O'Folliard was later charged individually for Robbery on May 1, 1879.[23]

Robert A. Widenman, a cowhand in the employ of John Tunstall and a clerk in his store, had a charge of Obstructing the Sheriff and Resisting an Officer.[24] Pantaleon Garcia had one murder charge lodged against him in Dona Ana County.[25] Most of the individuals participating in the Lincoln County War had numerous brushes with the law.

Two men controlled Lincoln Town and they were Lawrence G. Murphy and James J. Dolan. They owned the only store for miles around and farmers and ranchers had to sell their goods to them at deflated prices and credit (instead of money) was often extended to them in their store for merchandise sold at inflated prices. When the bill became large enough the two men would call the bill due. Since the customer could not pay the entire amount owed, his property would be taken away from him by the Murphy-Dolan controlled courts and resold by the two men. In many instances real estate would be resold without benefit of obtaining clear title in which cases the buyers would later lose the property to be resold once more by the men.

Charlie Bowdre and Dick Brewer both unwittingly bought ranches in this manner and the names of the ranches appear in the Lincoln County Commissioner's Minutes Books. Both men lost their property. When John Tunstall arrived in Lincoln he was offered a similar transaction but being forewarned of their game Tunstall declined. Alexander McSween was not the man he openly appeared to be. Though supposedly educated as a Presbyterian minister, according to Sue McSween, he is not in the records of the Presbyterian Historical Society nor does he appear in the **Ministerial Directory of the Presbyterian Church 1861-1941.** He only completed one year of a two year law course at Washington University in St. Louis and later became a schoolteacher and Justice of the Peace according to English historian Frederick Nolan. He went to work for Murphy and Dolan as a bookkeeper and later legal advisor though not a full-fledged lawyer.

He embezzled money from his employers as well as insurance money from one of their former partners and John Tunstall as well. Though he made a large sum of money from these enterprises he had financial difficulties of his own for in 1877 he sold a half-interest in his 10 room home to Sue McSween's sister Mrs. Elizabeth Shield. He was a man driven by greed and preferred to work on the money of others. Many civil charges appear in the court records between him, Murphy, Dolan, the Fritz family and others. When John Tunstall came to Lincoln he was taken in by McSween's pleasant countenance and impressed by his ambition. The two joined forces — on Tunstall's money.

Through McSween's influence Tunstall agreed to join him in breaking James J. Dolan who was the main power by the time the war had broken out as Major Murphy had retired to his ranch. They opened a general store in direct competition to the Murphy-Dolan one and when successful McSween was instrumental in getting Tunstall in incorporating a bank with $15,000 in capital assets — mostly Tunstall's. The loss of the money and business then set the stage for the Lincoln County War which would vault the then unknown Henry Antrim into national prominence. John Tunstall and Alexander McSween would both pay the price with their lives.

John Tunstall was the first to pay with his life and not only because he opposed the power in Lincoln but because he injured something far more important. Wherever money and power are to be had nothing shall stand in the way of its accumulation including human life. The root of such goals lie based in greed and there was more than enough greed in Lincoln to go around on both sides. With John Tunstall gone, John Chisum became the financial bank for all such operations openly and by distance. McSween was the main decision maker in Lincoln for the opposition.

McSween's greed knew no bounds. When John Tunstall was murdered McSween took the opportunity to write Tunstall's parents in England claiming that they were partners and that John died owing him large sums of money. Actually McSween had access to the accounts at banks in New York and St. Louis and when Tunstall died, Sue McSween may have gone to St. Louis to clean out the Tunstall account before it was closed. Mr. Tunstall had informed McSween that he might draw upon $25,000 in the First National Bank of New York City. Actually Mc-Sween already had access to this account and bank records disclose that he not only made the deposits but wrote the checks as well.

McSween acted as if he was unaware of this account he had been depositing and withdrawing money from for almost a year. From May 11, 1877 until November 10, 1877, he deposited $11,142.00. On August 23rd McSween withdrew $1,543.13 and another $1,000.00 on October 13th. McSween was supposed to use this money to bring John Tunstall's murderers to justice but most of it went into his own pocket.

The Tunstall cowhands were formed into a vigilante committee by McSween and they promptly named themselves the Regulators. This name was used many times on the frontier. The Regulators were, in actuality, an instrument of revenge and murder. The Regulators could not obtain legal arrest warrants through the district court or Justices of the Peace except for John B. "Squire" Wilson who was not under Murphy-Dolan control. Wilson issued them constable warrants for two individuals — Frank Baker and William Morton. Baker was a former companion of Henry Antrim in Mesilla but it is not known exactly where Morton came into the picture. Baker and Morton were chosen, presumably by McSween, to become the first victims of their revenge.

Morton and Baker had been present at the murder of John Tunstall. Although the Regulators were uncertain as to which of the opposing party had actually murdered Tunstall their identities were not of major importance at the moment, for all were scheduled to be exterminated. That the Morton and Baker murders were a prearranged contract to be paid for by or through McSween is a certain fact and it was not the last such contract. The Regulators got the constable's warrants for Morton and Baker for they already knew the two men were headed toward the area of the Chisum ranch.

The Regulators caught up with Morton and Baker riding with some other cowboys southward from the Chisum ranch area toward Seven Rivers when they spotted the Regulators and bolted away from the main party. The Regulators sought only the two men and pressed their pursuit in open, flat country. After a chase of undetermined length Morton and Baker were run to ground. After seeing escape was impossible and their situation hopeless they surrendered to what they knew must come. The regulators returned to the Chisum ranch where they spent the night before moving on toward Lincoln.

The party of Regulators were composed of eleven men. Present at this execution were Henry Antrim, Dick Brewer, J.G. "Doc" Scurlock, Charlie Bowdre, Henry Brown, Frank McNabb, Fred Waite (Wayte), Samuel Smith, James French, John Middleton and William McCloskey. Morton and Baker knew they were living their lives measured in minutes so when the party stopped by the Ash Upson store the following morning Morton borrowed some paper from Upson and wrote a letter to his cousin, H.H. Marshall in Virginia, warning them of his possible death.[29]

In this letter Morton named his executioners and for the first time the name of William Bonney comes into being. It will never be known whether Henry Antrim chose the name himself or whether it was given to him by someone else. If Henry chose it himself he had a stepfather named William H., a companion named William H. "Kid" Wilson, a friend named William H. Graham and in the next county a man named William Henry. The name of William H. brings up many conjectures but the name of Bonney is a complete mystery. One person claimed they called Henry "Henry Bonney" in Silver City but is unsupported by Henry's friends there.

This is as close to Bonney, Morton and Baker that Upson ever came. Upson posted the letter for Morton and the group departed for Lincoln. Though Upson never saw Morton and Baker after that, either dead or alive, he later claimed that he did in a letter home. This was printed in **Roswell In Its Early Years** by Maurice G. Fulton.

> My mind is full today of a horrible sight I witnessed day before yesterday, the body of the very worst, most beastly murderer this country ever saw dead, and mutilated in a most shocking manner. It would be treason to say I am sorry he was killed, but really I have enough Christian charity not to gloat or ever rejoice over any man's death. This fellow Frank Baker . . .

Upson then went on to relate a long story of Baker's past (perhaps fictional) glories and inglories. Also, in one of his letters he stated that three days after the posse and prisoners had departed his office (on March 11th) that he was surprised to see Frank McNabb (one of the posse members) entering his post office. Upson said that he remarked he thought that McNabb and party should be in Lincoln by this time. McNabb then gave him a fictitious tale of how "Morton grabbed a pistol from McCloskey and shot him dead," thus forcing the Regulators to kill both prisoners before anyone else was hurt or injured.

No one will ever know the full details of the executions but from what is known a great deal may be pieced together. As the party departed Upson's post office William Bonney and Charlie Bowdre were riding well in advance of the main party as lookouts and scouts. Nine men were left behind to guard the two unarmed prisoners. McCloskey was fully aware that their intentions were to murder the prisoners and protested loudly. He even went so far as to make the statement that in order to kill the prisoners they would have to kill him first. They did.

About halfway to Lincoln Bonney and Bowdre suddenly turned northward off the main road toward what is known as Blackwater Holes. The main body then followed suit. When this occured Baker and Morton became alarmed and McNabb rode up behind McCloskey and shot him through the head, killing him instantly. This became the signal for what then followed.

There were now eight men left in the posse and as soon as the first man killed McCloskey the remaining seven fired one bullet apiece into the bodies of their hapless victims.* Because of the distance involved and the split-second timing Bonney and Bowdre did not, and could not, participate. The firing of a single bullet by each member of the immediate party present was a communal, shared responsibility that would benefit each individual, perhaps by money offered him through Alexander McSween. This was but the first occurrence of the shared-guilt-responsibility killing. It soon would surface again in the killing of Sheriff Brady but that time there would be witnesses to the offer made by Alexander McSween.

The bodies were not mutilated as suggested by Upson, but left where they fell as a warning to the opposition. Some sheepherders were the first to discover the corpses and they were quickly buried beneath piles of stones thus cancelling Upson's statement that he had seen the bodies. He was unaware of the murders until McNabb told him three days later.

The second shared murder occurred on April 1, 1878, and had a far more serious goal in mind than just eliminating the opposition. William Brady was sheriff under the control of the Murphy-Dolan dominated courts of Lincoln County although he was not always in compliance nor agreement with what they were doing and their actions. But because he was the sheriff he had the power of life and death over the Regulators as well as the authority to arrest them for any wrongdoing. He became an enemy simply because he was an authority figure.

Brady had been issued warrants by the controlled court for Alexander McSween and at the time of his death he was carrying two of them

*The wounds vary from source to source but 8 is generally accepted. This, like the Sheriff Brady murder, was an execution, and since they were offered $500 each to kill Brady it is more than likely that that was also.

64

in his inside coat pocket as he had expected to serve them that very morning when McSween showed up for the April term of court. One was for his arrest and the other was to attach his cattle. McSween departed Lincoln and hid out east of Roswell in order to protect himself and would not allow himself to be taken into custody by the opposing faction. Without him the Regulators would be leaderless for Chisum would do nothing. Besides, he would lose all the cattle herd he had built up on the money of others. Either way he lost.

According to a witness, McSween convinced the Regulators that they could not allow Brady to arrest him.* This would also place each and every Regulator in certain jeopardy as well their employment. Being a lawyer of sorts, McSween was aware that only one warrant was ever issued in every case and should anything happen to that warrant he could not be arrested nor lose his cattle. That was the law. It would take a delay of at least until the following term of District Court to reissue duplicate warrants and that would certainly buy time for McSween. If McSween were removed from the picture the opposition would fold for John Chisum was not brave enought to take the responsibility of command and thus place his own saftey in a precarious position. Therefore McSween's orders were for the Regulators to execute Sheriff Brady on the morning McSween would appear which was a week prior to the April term of court and retrieve the two warrants he carried in his inside coat pocket. McSween had already told Brady he would appear that day.

In order to give them incentive to do the job and to keep from being neutralized through McSween's removal, John Chisum offered to pay each participating man in the affair the sum total of $500 a piece. Though McSween was to appear that morning he would delay long enough to give his men time to complete their dastardly task.

The Regulators then made open threats against the life of District Court Judge Warren Bristol and other court officials so Bristol decided not to hold the April term of court.† The decision was made shortly before court was to convene. Brady was known to be in Lincoln that morning for he supposedly had stayed overnight instead of riding in from his ranch 3 miles east of town. The problem facing the Regulators was how to get Brady out into the open so he might be slain. The Regulators had originally planned to ambush Brady that morning on his way from his ranch but now they had to somehow lure him into the open streets of Lincoln.

*For a complete and documented account see **Sheriff William Brady, Tragic Hero of the Lincoln County War**, by Donald R. Lavash.

†By law or custom the term of court was always the second Monday of April.

It was decided to send one of their members to a local store in the east end where he would pretend to be drunk and disorderly. Brady would be summoned and would have to ride directly due east past the position previously chosen by the Regulators to intercept him. A man was dispatched to fetch Brady (at either the courthouse or Dolan store) to come and remove the person causing the disturbance.*

Brady departed the building and mounted his blooded Arabian sorrel mare branded BB on the left hip and with both ears split. Unfortunately, at the final moment Deputy George Hindeman, George Peppin, John Long and Billy Matthews decided to ride along and finish their conversation. It would be the final ride for Brady and Hindeman.

The men rode at a leisurely walk eastward toward a curve in front of the Tunstall store. Behind the adobe wall of the store on the east side of the building were approximately 12 men or so who lay in wait. The exact figure is uncertain. It did not displease Bonney that Billy Matthews was in the group for Bonney and Matthews were sworn enemies and, as it turned out, apparently only Bonney singled out Matthews as his victim. The remainder would concentrate on Brady and Hindeman. The men would be hidden from view from the lawmen until the final moment by the east wall of the Tunstall store. They would have only a few moments to sight and fire. A multitude of rifle barrels protruded over the wall and suddenly a volley of explosions rent the still morning air.

Brady and Hindeman tumbled from their saddles immediately as the men fired shots into each of their prostrate forms.† Brady had died instantly for he never moved afterwards. However, Hindeman's hand moved only slightly once before he silently expired.‡ Billy Matthews was miraculously spared untouched except for one individual who kept firing at him as he spurred his horse forward and out of sight. Bonney was the only man of the group that failed to place a bullet into either corpse. With Brady and Hindeman down and Matthews riding for his life Bonney and James French vaulted the wall and approached the still bodies to remove the warrants. By now the streets were full of onlookers and Bonney and French were oblivious of the citizenry looking on. It did not matter to them that now both could be plainly identified as being in the murder party for this was insignificant in lieu of what they had to gain.

*All accounts state that Brady stayed in his office that night but the Brady family stated that he rode into town that morning.

†The number of wounds in the bodies varies from writer to writer but eight is generally accepted. The Brady family said they counted 16 holes but this would include exit holes. He was shot once under the left arm in the side.

‡Some writers have claimed that Hindeman crawled a short distance and asked for water but eyewitnesses stated that he never moved or spoke save for a slight twitch of one hand.

By that time Matthews had dismounted and taken refuge inside a deep doorway where he stood half-hidden from view. When Bonney and French appeared Matthews took aim and fired. Before Matthews could fire, Bonney had already rolled Brady onto his back and was reaching into his inside coat pocket when the first shot caught him a glancing blow across the hip. A second ball struck French in the breast and passed out the back but neither man went down. Bonney already had one warrant in his grasp when he felt that discretion was the better part of valor and decided to retreat. With Matthews having a clear line of fire, Bonney quickly saw that the only way to shield himself and French was behind Brady's horse so he caught the animal with one hand and walked them both to safety behind the animal. Matthews did not fire again for fear of hitting the horse. The horse was a valuable one and Bonney was to keep it in his possession for the next seven months.

Many writers, unaware of the important documents within Brady's coat pocket, have attempted to explain that Bonney was simply after Brady's pistol or rifle, depending on which version you prefer to accept.* In later years George Coe attempted to cover his part in the execution and hide the fact that the participants were paid to commit the deed by simply repeating what unlearned writers had already given him as an escape.

Neither Bonney nor French were foolish enough to try and risk their lives and openly display their indentities to the entire town of Lincoln for a rifle or pistol they could buy anywhere new for $12.00 or less for a used one with a horse standing by that was worth more than six times what either weapon was worth and even then it was an afterthought of necessity. They were after something far more important than a cheap gun. They had one of Brady's warrants.

Some writers say that the number of bullets in each slain man's body totaled eleven — the same number of men in the party except for Bonney who was firing at Matthews. Sue McSween later stated that Bonney had told her he was shooting at Matthews. Pat Garrett backed up this statement with his admission that Bonney had told him the same thing. This was said in a conversation to Governor Miguel Otero also.

Bonney was suffering from a nasty wound in the hip, James French would survive his serious wound and John B. "Squire" Wilson had accidentally taken an embarassing flesh wound in the buttock by a wildly discharged shot. Two hours later McSween and John Chisum rode into the lower end of Lincoln in a buggy. There was a large crowd still gathered about the two bodies that still lay in the street but both men

*The Brady family stated that Sheriff Brady had purchased a new rifle about three weeks previous.

rode on by without even glancing in their direction to ascertain what had happened and to whom. They did not need to for they already knew.

William Bonney was charged in causes 243 and 244 for the twin murders and for the first time he was charged under the now-famous alias of William Bonney alias Kid alias William Antrim.[27] Although the arrest warrant for William Bonney was issued only three days later his indictments had to wait for twenty-two days until after the Grand Jury met. None of the Regulators ever collected a penny of the money promised them for the Brady murder from Chisum although McSween had had many times that amount in the First National Bank in New York City. Neither did McSween attempt to pay them.

This is why William Bonney so often made the statement that John Chisum owed him $500 and that he (Bonney) intended to collect it one way or another. Why else would a wealthy cattleman owe such a large amount to a $20.00 a month cowhand that didn't even work for him?

What is ironic about the entire affair is that when the war came to an end all participants save William Bonney left New Mexico and never had to stand trial for a single crime. Only Bonney was foolish enough to remain behind and he alone would stand trial and be convicted of two murders he did not commit. He was guilty only of being an accessory but he was the only one of the Regulators the Territory of New Mexico had in its possession and they decided to make an example of him.

To make the statement that William Bonney was overly cautious when it came to his personal safety would be something of an understatement. It was a religion with him.

During the battle of the McSween home which ended the war his animalistic instinct for survival once again saved his life. The house was finally set afire and slowly the flames ate through the 10 room adobe home. An hour later, while the flames ate away at the structure, Robert Beckwith approached the front of the house and called for McSween to surrender the house and all within it. McSween stood in the doorway with several other men speaking to Beckwith when several of the men suddenly fired on Beckwith, killing him instantly. Beckwith was shot twice in the head and once in the wrist according to the Coroner's Jury Report. While modern day writers prefer to lay this killing (as well as every other death in Lincoln County it seems) at the doorstep of William Bonney, he had not fired a shot at Beckwith.

The Coroner's Jury made the statement that Harvey Morris, Zamora and several unidentified Mexicans were guilty along with the unarmed Alexander McSween. McSween had never carried a weapon and during the three-day seige of his home had repeatedly refused to pick up a weapon and defend his own life though repeatedly asked to do so.

Whether he gave his men the order to fire or not is lost to history. His very being in the doorway made him guilty for it was McSween and McSween only that the Dolan-controlled mob was after.

When the flames began to reach the 10th room it was time for all to make their move to preserve their lives or end it. McSween was among the first, if not the first, to step out into the light of the dancing flames that night. There are conflicting stories as to what occured next but it is certain that McSween fell with five bullets in his body and fell near Beckwith's corpse. As the others dashed out it became a slaughter. The boy-Robin Hood, William Bonney, remained true to his nature and allowed everyone else to enter the charnel yard. While the attention of the opposition was focused upon the hapless targets coming out a single door Bonney waited his chance and then dashed out. He went toward the Tunstall store but soldiers from Fort Stanton stationed there fired on him. He veered to his left, vaulted the low fence near the five, still bodies and disappeared into the darkness along the Bonito River.

The Lincoln County War was ended. The Regulators were no more. Though Bonney was still virtually unknown and a minor figure of that war at this precise moment of time future writers would soon glorify him into the God that he was not and certainly did not deserve to be. Even Governor Wallace thought so little of Bonney's accomplishments that he ranked the outlaw only 14th on the most wanted list of the territory.

The **Grant County Herald** gave their version of the battle and agreed that McSween, Morris, Zamora and others had killed Beckwith. [28] The surviving Regulators were now leaderless, unemployed and totally without direction. They were still unable to collect the monies owed them by Chisum for their paid execution of Sheriff Brady who felt his finanical obligations ended with the death of McSween or perhaps he never intended to pay them. He pulled out, never to return. He never honored his debt to the Regulators.

Most of the men simply shrugged it off, chalked it up to experience and departed the country — except for William Bonney who allowed it to become a cancer that would eat away at him for the remainder of his brief life.

The unemployed outlaws, left to their own devices, now turned fulltime to the only manner of living that they knew. Though many had been outlaws prior to the war, most had continued to practice their profession to some extent while the war was in progress. Bonney was born to steal and he found it a pleasurable manner to earn a living.

"The Kid," a boy who was arrested for stealing horses from Cal Hunter, and the rest, just as bad characters. [29]

James J. Dolan had not let up on the destruction of the Regulators, he intended to destroy or drive them from the Territory. He wrote a letter to the **Santa Fe New Mexican** concerning William Bonney and defined his character as such: "I will state here that Wm. H. Antrim, 'alias the kid,' a renegade from Arizona, where he killed a man in cold blood, Waite from Indian Territory . . ."[30]

Dolan's allegations only enhanced the Bonney reputation which would soon be blown out of proportion thanks to the help of local news reporters. He quickly became known as a petty horse, mule and cattle thief across two states. In October of 1878 he began to expand his theater of operations into the Texas Panhandle where he soon became as unwanted as in New Mexico. Outside of these two locales he was virtually unknown to the remainder of the country. Even to the large newspapers. Just how large an area he covered in Texas was surprising.

Few historians know that Bonney's name also appeared three times in the Lincoln County Commissioner's Minutes book. Isaac Ellis presented an account against Lincoln County for "the board of William Bonnie and Thomas O'Folliard" and for the care and feeding of their horses. The bill came to a total of $64.00. Samuel R. Corbett presented a second bill for the "boarding of W. Bonnie and Thomas O'Folliard and J.G. 'Doc' Scurlock" in the amount of $150.00. John B. "Squire" Wilson, a former Regulator himself, added his own bill against the county for services rendered in holding a coroner's inquest upon the bodies of J.H. Tunstall $3.00; A.A. McSween $3.00; Vicente Romero $3.00; Harvey Morris $3.00; Frank Zamora $3.00; Robert Beckwith $3.00; Bito Becalo $3.00 and H. Chapman $3.00.[31]

All of the above corpses were victims of the McSween house battle excepting H.J. Chapman, attorney for Mrs. McSween, who was murdered by William Campbell and James J. Dolan while William Bonney was forced to look on while being held captive by Jesse Evans.[32]

Bonney found fresh fields to conquer in the northernmost portion of Texas known as the Panhandle. Maps of 400 years ago called this area the **Gran Quivara.** Later it became known as "The Great American Desert" and finally, in due time, it became The Staked Plains. Coronado explored it in 1541 as the first European on the plains and Canadian River Valley area and was followed in 1599 by Juan de Onate. It was Comanche country but the buffalo hunters came anyway and were soon followed by the ranchers, farmers, and settlers. Inevitably the outlaw and criminal element was swift in appearing.

In the late 1870's there were but three towns in existence in the Panhandle country. Mobeetie began in 1875, Tascosa in 1876 and Clarenden in 1878. Mobeetie was originally known as "Hide Town" due to the buffalo hunting trade. Later the name was changed to Sweetwater and finally to Mobeetie. G.J. Howard and Ira J. Rinehart came from Elizabethtown, New Mexico, in 1877 to establish a two room adobe store in Tascosa. Howard later left to begin his own establishment with James E. McMasters of Taos, New Mexico.

James McMasters was then 34 years of age, unmarried and a native of Pennsylvania. Ira Rinehart was age 37 years, widowed and a native of Ohio. Living with him was his 13 year old son Irvin.[33]

The Howard and McMaster's store was a one floor adobe with double doors on the front and three windows. Tascosa consisted only of the Howard and McMaster's store, Rinehart's, a blacksmith shop and an adobe house. Most of the lots were later owned by G.J. Howard and Jim McMasters. They refused to sell newcomer John Cone a lot as he desired to open a competing store so he went a half-mile down river and settled on a lot purchased from Casmero Romero. A red light district came later. Old Tascosa died in the middle 1890's.

The Panhandle was perfect cattle country and totally open range. The largest ranch was the XIT which had a 200 mile grazing range. The sprawling LX was about 20 miles north of present day Amarillo and the LIT was equally large. There were many other smaller ranchers and William Bonney overlooked none of them.

There was no law in the Panhandle until 1881 and this made it an ideal country for the likes of William Bonney. There were no courthouses and they used the Clay County courthouse at Henrietta in north Texas. In order to file a complaint the rancher would have ride several hundred miles to Henrietta to the courthouse, file a complaint and then return. A busy rancher did not have the time to waste and they usually handled such matters of importance in their own way. They simply killed the offender. Counties never filed the complaint; it had to be handled by the injured party. There were three major bands of horse and cattle thieves. John Selman was alleged to have some 175 men and worked from the Canadian River to Devil's River. Dutch Henry had about the same number of men but Charlie Siringo claimed he had as many as 300. William Bonney had the smallest band that never exceeded 10-15 men at any given time.[34] There were only 192 people listed in Oldham County during the 1880 census report.[35]

Bonney's first visit to the Panhandle was reasonably well-documented by Dr. Henry F. Hoyt in his book **Frontier Doctor**. This occured in October of 1878. Bonney's reputation for throwing a loose rope was already well-known to the ranchers in Oldham County for his reputation had long preceded him. When Bonney arrived the ranchers held a meeting and invited Bonney to attend. He was informed in a blunt manner that they knew who he was and as long as he behaved himself he would have no trouble, otherwise . . .

Bonney would behave himself in Tascosa, as did his men, but each time he departed he left in the company of someone else's cattle. He arrived with approximately 125 head of stolen horses — all wearing mixed brands. He sold his horses and caused no trouble. However, he lost many of his men who decided to quit in Tascosa. Some remained as cowhands in the Tascosa area like Kid Dobbs and Charles Reasor while others like Henry Brown, Fred Waite, John Middleton departed for other locations.

Kid Dobbs and Charles Reasor went to work for local ranchers as did another member known only as Mortimer because it was more than they were making stealing cattle. At that time a cowboy could eventually build his own herd as they were allowed to capture and brand as their own any unbranded cattle they chanced to find on the range. The rancher allowed them to keep their herd on his property thus enabling many a poor cowpoke to start a herd of his own. This all changed in the 1880's.

Bonney and Hoyt became unlikely friends and before Hoyt departed for Las Vegas, New Mexico, Bonney allowed Hoyt to ride a horse named Dandy Dick that Hoyt had been admiring. According to the Hoyt version Bonney "gave" him the horse **gratis** and wrote out a bill of sale for $75.00 to protect Hoyt if he ever needed to prove ownership. It is illogical that Bonney gave anyone such a valuable animal for it was the most valuable animal that Bonney ever owned and worth more than the $75.00 shown on the bill of sale. The horse was a blooded Arabian, branded BB on the left hip and had both ears split.

In 1924, after rising to national prominence, Hoyt wrote the Lincoln County Courthouse asking the original ownership of the animal which verified that he knew it was stolen and that he knew where the horse had come from. Sheriff Brady's son identified the horse as being the one taken by Bonney after his father was murdered.

Bonney risked his life for this valuable animal and had kept it with him for seven months while moving about constantly, always on the run and one step ahead of a rope. I do not accept the excuse that Bonney "gave" the horse to Hoyt. The circumstances imply that Hoyt simply purchased the animal. Hoyt had good reason to claim the horse was a gift for by 1924 he had risen to the position of Surgeon-General of the United States and had a reputation to protect. It was not illegal to purchase a stolen animal for all the law required was a bill of sale to prove your ownership, not the previous owner's. There is no further evidence in Bonney's lifetime that he ever gave away anything of value.

When Bonney departed Tascosa in late October he rounded up the Panhandle cattle and took them back to New Mexico and sold them. This became his method of operation the remainder of his life. It was a short ride of a few days from the eastern side of New Mexico to anywhere within the Panhandle area. It was two days from Tascosa to Las Vegas. From New Mexico he could venture up to the Oklahoma border in the Panhandle down to Lubbock, Midland, Odessa, San Angelo and Pecos areas as they were all closer than Tascosa. It is known that he frequently made these trips. There are large gaps of missing time in Bonney's life where he could have been in west Texas, the Panhandle and Old Mexico. People in those days traveled long distances by horseback and gave no thought to it.

Bonney's cowardly disposition and inflated ego were evident in his relations with a 70 year old Tascosa rancher named Ellsworth Torrey. Bonney had hit Torrey's herds heavily and Torrey was aware of this fact. One night Bonney's men, minus their leader, appeared at the Torrey ranch and demanded to be fed. The Torreys cooked them a meal, as was the custom on the range then, but the outlaws were so rude and discourteous that Mr. Torrey angrily chased them off his property. They immediately told Bonney.[36]

A few days following the incident Torrey appeared in Tascosa and Bonney saw his chance to enchance his reputation at the expense of an old, frightened and unarmed man and approached him. Bonney took out his pistol, cocked it and placed it against Torrey's chest demanding a public apology for his men. The frightened old man complied and Bonney added to his reputation at Torrey's expense. Some writers claim that it frightened Torrey so that he quit the country and went back north but this is not so. Torrey remained in Tascosa and did not remove himself until a year after Bonney was dead and then for his own reasons.

A study of the murders Bonney was involved in or participated in shows his own personal lack of courage. As a young boy in Silver City he pulled a pocketknife on an unarmed blacksmith. Thomas Moore was drunk and unarmed and Cahill was likewise unsuspecting. Brady and Hindeman were shot from ambush without warning and Robert Olinger's death was a similar setup. J.W. Bell was unarmed and fleeing when murdered and Joe Grant was the crowning glory of the coward.

Bonney was afraid of many men, including Jesse Evans, and greatly feared Dave Rudabaugh who was perhaps the most cold-blooded killer that Bonney had ever known. Bonney always maintained a low profile around these men when in their presence. There is not a single instance of Bonney ever going up against an armed individual or someone of equal or better reputation. He always fought the coward's fight.

Many people felt that Bonney's only visit to Texas was in October of 1878 when, in actuality, Panhandle history discloses that he was a frequent but unwanted visitor. In September of 1878 Charles and Frank Sperling took over the old, abandoned Trujillo Plaza in western Oldham County and it became a popular stage stop between Las Vegas and Tascosa. John Atkins later built a hotel there. The Sperlings had trouble with Bonney and his men during the two year period Bonney drifted back and forth into the Texas Panhandle.

Bonney was in most of the Panhandle counties at one time or another as well as parts of west Texas as far down as Pecos and possibly into the San Angelo, Odessa-Midland and Lubbock areas as well. A search of the Panhandle criminal records over a span of several years has failed to turn up a single criminal docket book but it is doubtful that any charges would be discovered in them.

Though Bonney was the most notorious cattle, horse and mule thief in Lincoln County no charges were ever filed against him by that county or neighboring San Miguel during the Lincoln County War or afterwards. San Miguel County did file charges against him for Keeping a Gaming Table. Finally, in May of 1880 Bernalillo County (Albuquerque) filed two charges of Stealing a Mare against him. It was a usual thing not to file charges against a known criminal for fear of your own safety.

Though the newspapers reported that he was arrested for stealing horses from Cal Hunter, no charge was brought against him. When the Las Vegas authorities arrested him for a brief period he was allowed to go free although Lincoln County had several outstanding murder warrants against him that were well-known to them. This indifference extended into his Panhandle and west Texas forays.

After his former companion-in-crime Jesse Evans was captured in Texas, reports reached the Texas Rangers that William Bonney and a group of outlaws numbering some 15 or 20 men had been depredating that area for some time around the Pecos Crossing (also known as the immigrant's crossing from earlier days) which was between Fort Stockton and present day San Angelo in Greene County. The Ranger report spoke of him as "W. Antrim, alias 'Billie the Kid'." Ranger Captain Charles L. Nevill arrived in Fort Stockton to check with the local authorities in order to obtain arrest warrants for Bonney and his men but Fort Stockton authorities could not confirm nor deny the rumors from the settlers around the Pecos Crossing area for all refused to talk for fear of their lives.

At the Pecos Crossing area there were approximately 200 people living there and none would be brave enough to put his name on a complaint against Bonney for, if arrested, he had at least 20 men still at large to cause harm to the settlers and their families. Nevill was forced to return emptyhanded. [37]

Over the years, descendants of pioneer families of early Panhandle and west Texas settlers have told of his visits and his thefts. Many of these settlers had fed Bonney and his men from time to time, including the ones he was stealing cattle from.

Since there were but three towns in the entire Panhandle in 1880 it would seem more than certain that Bonney also visited all of them. This includes Mobeetie and Clarenden. In order to sell stolen cattle and horses it would be necessary for him to have visited the areas of population as he did at Tascosa. The remainder of the land was vast, open prairie sparsely settled by an occasional ranch house. The first law in the Panhandle came to Mobeetie and one of its deputies was John W. Poe. Poe later stated in his book that he did not know what Bonney looked like the night he accompanied Pat Garrett to the Pete Maxwell house in 1881 but he certainly must have known him by reputation, which was known across the Panhandle.

The ranchers were losing so much cattle to the lawless element that they were forced to form a cattleman's association in order to protect themselves from such huge losses. The hapless ranchers met at Mobeetie in 1880 and formed the Panhandle Stock Association of Texas. They offered a reward of $250 for anyone caught rustling association cattle. The also had their own lawmen.

They hired men like Pat Garrett and John W. Poe to end the reign of such outlaws as William Bonney, Dutch Henry and John Selman. The large Panhandle ranchers had previously sent some of their own cowhands, many former associates of Bonney, after the young outlaw, but they were too few in number to effect a solution to the problem and they lacked any legal authority when they crossed the New Mexico line. After all, they were not professional lawmen but cowhands and former outlaws. They were not willing to risk their lives for cattle that was not their own, therefore the Association needed professional, dedicated men.

Though Dutch Henry and John Selman certainly had larger operations it was William Bonney they first went after, which gives an indication of how many times he crossed into the Panhandle and how often and hard he hit the unguarded herds.

Though Garrett was a former acquaintance of Bonney (and this is one of the reasons for his selection) he owed Bonney nothing and was willing to end the young outlaw's career in any manner he could. As for John Poe he was merely doing his duty without any involved emotion. Poe's only contact with Bonney was the night Poe was sitting on the front porch of Pete Maxwell's house when Bonney suddenly came striding unexpectedly out of the darkness, sans boots and pistol, seeking the side of smoked beef that he understood was hanging there.

Poe made the statement that he didn't recognize Bonney as he had never seen him before. Even so, Bonney was almost unrecognizable with his newly-grown beard and stained skin. When the figure spoke to him in Spanish Poe took him to be just another one of Maxwell's employees and attempted to calm any fears he might have by informing him they were there on business to see Maxwell. Though Poe failed to recognize him, Garrett did not and took the opportunity to cut short Bonney's rope.

The LS Ranch a few miles south of Tascosa lost many head of cattle to Bonney over a two year period as had the LX near present-day Amarillo, Mr. Torrey and countless other ranchers both large and small including the mammoth XIT and LIT spreads. The losses suffered by the ranchers at the hands of the rustlers became tremendous so the cattle men set about handling the situation to their own satisfaction.

Though Dutch Henry, John Selman and countless others raided the Panhandle herds, they took their booty and departed in secrecy, while Bonney boldly rode into these areas, sold his stolen New Mexico horses openly, then brazenly stole the cattle of his former customers. Bonney flaunted his thievery in their faces.

The first expedition of cowboys sent out to cut Bonney short was a group headed by Frank Stewart. Frank Stewart was a detective for the stock association and he took four men along with him. Kid Dobbs and Charley Reasor of the LIT were former companions of Bonney. They had arrived in Tascosa in October of 1878 and decided to stay. They went to work for less but steadier pay and a longer life span. A cowhand's pay wasn't much but it was sufficient since the money received from stolen cattle had to be divided many ways.

Kid Dobbs represented the James Campbell cattle outfit and Reasor the LIT. They were joined by Lee Hall and Lon Chambers of the LX ranch. Only Stewart had any experience in such matters and they were poorly equipped for the expedition they were undertaking. In the fall of 1880 they rode out of Tascosa and followed the trail of Bonney back into New Mexico Territory.

They headed for White Oaks and once there came immediately upon a corral fence covered with the drying hides of cattle bearing the LIT brand. LIT cattle wore this brand on the right side and a large U was burned on the left side of the neck. Only Dobbs and Reasor were aware that Bonney sold much of his stolen cattle in White Oaks and that no one bothered him there. Jim Greathouse bought a lot as did the Dedrick brothers and Pat Coghlan further westward. The remainder went to butchershops, ranchers and other individuals.

Upon questioning the butcher quickly produced a legal bill of sale from Bonney for the stolen cattle. Such sales were legal under

Territorial laws so there was nothing the Texas group could do about it. The butcher was aware the cattle were stolen and he knew William Bonney and had undoubtedly purchased similar stock over the years. He claimed to have made the purchase "in good faith" and since he had the required bill of sale he intended on selling the meat and keeping the hides.

Later two local merchants approached Stewart and informed him that Bonney and ten of his men had been in White Oaks three days previous, taking everything that they wanted from local merchants without bothering to pay for it or even to charge it. The merchants knew full well the group had no intentions of paying for anything. This was another example of how Bonney preferred to live off the sweat of honest men. [43]

Since the Bonney faction outnumbered the Texas group by more than two to one, the merchants felt that if the two groups should meet the Texas men would receive the worst of it.

Dobbs and Reasor felt that Bonney would not hurt them if the meeting did not involve shooting but if Bonney feared for his safety, he was not known for his loyalty to his former comrades. They declined to run the risk of a head-on confrontation and returned to the Panhandle without further incident. There must have been other such futile attempts to capture William Bonney.

In 1880 Garrett headed the only successful pursuit of William H. Bonney. Garrett was hired by the association to enter New Mexico and capture or kill Bonney and put an end to his continuing thefts. In order to divert suspicion from their true intent they were to tell everyone they encountered that they were simply after drift cattle that had strayed across the Texas line into New Mexico. The utmost secrecy was required in order that Bonney sympathizers not learn of their mission and inform their quarry. This group was much larger than the previous group (or groups) and much better financed. The party was composed of cowhands from LX, LIT, LS, Torrey and a smattering of others — all victims of the Bonney greed.

Included in this posse was the celebrated Charlie Siringo. Pat Garrett was the only one familiar with Bonney's habits, personality and most of his favorite haunts and friends. Garrett was now sheriff of Lincoln County and had sworn to rid the country of its unwanted elements, particulary William Bonney as he was the last of the Lincoln outlaws. These efforts finally culminated in success for Garrett when he successfully ambushed the Bonney party late one night at Fort Sumner which resulted in the death of Tom O'Folliard who died in Bonney's place. Charlie Bowdre was killed the following morning and the remainder

77

taken captive.

Garrett was aware of the cowardly nature of his prey and he knew that as long as Bonney was aware that they were in the vicinity he would remain hidden. Should word reach Bonney that the Garrett posse had left he would boldly resurface to reestablish his image to those about him and to feed his growing ego.

Garrett was aware that all of the Bonney men were single save for Charlie Bowdre and that Bowdre's wife, Manuela, lived in a room in the old Fort Sumner hospital. Bowdre was certain to come visit her as soon as the coast was clear. Garrett had the word spread about that he was frightened of being ambushed and that his posse had left Fort Sumner for safer parts. The brash Bonney nature would not allow him to pass up a golden opportunity to take advantage of such a situation. Garrett's psychology proved to be correct.

When Bonney heard the news that Garrett had fled he immediately began to cast slurs upon their lack of courage. Fort Sumner now appeared to be safe so Charlie could go to town and visit his wife. That night, around midnight, Bonney led his men through the softly falling snow toward the old post hospital. As he approached, his automatic sense of self-preservation told him to be cautious. It might be a trap. He told O'Folliard that he needed some tobacco and excused himself to ride to the rear of the party in case something should happen. It wasn't long in coming.

O'Folliard was selected to be the sacrificial goat and rode up upon the Garrett party submerged in the shadows taking the first bullet meant for Bonney. At the sound of the first shots Bonney made no attempt to return the fire but immediately whirled his mount and left his men behind to fend for themselves. He fired not one shot in his defense. They could not remain at the ranch where they had been hiding out for it might now be known to Garrett so they picked up their things and rode to the old Alejandro Perea cabin located on the north side of Arroyo Taiban, known locally as Stinking Springs. Pat and his men followed their tracks in the glistening snow and set up a line of defense immediately in front of the cabin door and behind them along an L-shaped hill. The cabin had a single door facing the arroyo in the southeast corner of the cabin wall that faced the posse. The outlaws had made a grave mistake — they had left their horses outside tied to the rafters.

Some versions state that Garrett gave orders to shoot Bonney the moment he stepped through the door but since Garrett had no way of knowing who would come out the door first, he probably told them to shoot the first man out the door and immediately establish their domination of the situation and gain a psychological edge over the outlaws. If

Bonney remained true to his pursuit of self-preservation he would not be the first man out of the door. Bonney had been ambushed only hours before and since Garrett was still in the vicinity it was possible that he might be waiting for them the following morning.

It is equally foolish to claim that the posse mistook Charlie Bowdre for William Bonney the following morning. Though both men were of the same general size and build Bowdre was a man of 32 years of age, had a large mass of hair and always wore a big mustache, while Bonney was younger, clean-shaven and had less hair. If orders were given to shoot, and they most certainly were, what would the posse be expected to do if someone other than Bonney walked out of the door or all came out firing at once? There would be no chance of selection. It was simple, straightforward and logical reasoning on Garrett's part. Shoot the first man, or men, out the door, reduce their numbers immediately and dominate them by reason of surprise.

Bonney slyly talked Bowdre into going outside and feeding the horses while he remained safely inside. Bowdre picked up the feed bags and stepped out the cabin door into the bright sunlight. A volley split the frozen silence and seven bullets struck Bowdre at once, one cutting his elastic suspenders and popping the metal clip onto the snow.[45] Amazingly Bowdre did not fall but remained erect and staggered back into the cabin leaking his lifeblood along the way.

Bonney was not certain that they were surrounded and for no other reason than his bad disposition he decided to sacrifice his close friend of the past two years. He moved Bowdre's pistol around to the front of his body and Garrett's men could clearly hear his voice as he told the dying Bowdre to go out and take some of Garrett's men with him. Two or three less lawmen would enhance Bonney's chances of escape. Garrett saw no profit in killing a dead man and ordered his men to hold their fire. Bowdre walked out to collapse in their arms whispering, "I wish. . .I wish."

Though Bonney and Garrett talked back and forth to each other during the course of the day Bonney was not the one brave enough to come out and talk with the lawmen. It was the braver Dave Rudabaugh who presented his body to the posse while Bonney remained safely inside after failing in his attempt to ride his faithful horse over the dead body of the horse the lawmen had shot in the cabin doorway to prevent such an occurrence. Garrett had forseen this possibility almost immediately and shot away the reins of the other mounts while dropping one dead in the doorway.

Bonney always lived in fear of those he felt were his equal or better and although he feared Jesse Evans he held more fear for Dave

Rudabaugh who was already established as a ruthless, cold-blooded killer. It was Rudabaugh's courage that sent him outside to make arrangements for their surrender for they were in a hopeless situation, while the famous Bonney remained safe behind stone walls. It was Dave Rudabaugh that commanded the situation and it was Rudabaugh that conducted the surrender arrangements. Bonney had played a minor role.

The gang, hungry and tired, saw no other recourse but to surrender. Their horses were gone, they had no food or water and they were entirely surrounded by a group of men that were more than willing to send them on the same journey Charlie Bowdre had taken. Once again William H. Bonney was delivered into the arms of the law — but not for long.

NOTES
CHAPTER 4

1. 1880 census for Mesilla, Dona Ana County.
2. Las Cruces **Thirty-Four**, March 26, 1879.
3. Las Cruces **Thirty-Four**, January 22, 1879.
4. Ibid.
5. **Thirty-Four**, January 29, 1879.
6. 1880 Census Report, Dona Ana County, town of Mesilla.
7. Dona Ana Criminal Docket Book, 1877-1883.
8. Lincoln County Criminal Docket Book, 1879, cause #298.
9. Reverse Index to Criminal Records, U.S. District Court, El Paso, charge #297, p. 276.
10. Dona Ana Criminal Docket Books 1875-1879. Lincoln County Criminal Docket Books 1877-1878. Pecos County Docket Book, April 21, 1880.
11. Dona Ana Civil & Criminal Docket Books 1875-1880.
12. **Thirty-Four**, Wed., January 1, 1879.
13. **Thirty-Four**, Wed., Feb. 12, 1879.
14. **Thirty-Four**, Wed., May 12, 1879.
15. **Mesilla Independant,** October 13, 1877. The Oct. 20 issue stated that Ledbetter's horse turned up in the possession of Jesse Evans.
16. **The Boyhood of Billy the Kid,** by Robert N. Mullin.
17. Office of the Civil Archives in Washington. General Services Administration letter dated September 29, 1964.
18. 1880 census, Fort Sumner and vicinity, page 435.
19. Descendants of early Fort Sumner families.
20. **Frontier Fighter,** by George Coe. 1964 conversation with C.G. Silva, grandson of Jesus Silva — a friend of William Bonney.
21. Letter of W.H. Graham's daughter Gertrude Graham Butler dated September 25, 1963.
22. Lincoln County Brands Book. McSween registered the)(brand.
23. Lincoln County Criminal Docket Book A, April 21, 1879.
24. Dona Ana County Criminal Docket Record, Nov. 20, 1878 to April 23, 1881.
25. Dona Ana County Criminal Docket Record, Nov. 20, 1878 to April 14, 1879.
26. Letter of William S. Morton to his cousin H.H. Marshall dated March 8, 1878.
27. Lincoln County Criminal Docket Book A, Eighth Day, Tues., April 22, 1878, pp. 318 and 330.
28. **Grant County Herald,** August 3, 1878.
29. **Santa Fe New Mexican,** Saturday, April 30, 1878. No charges were ever filed against him for this theft.
30. **Santa Fe New Mexican,** May 25, 1878.
31. Lincoln County Commissioner's Minutes Book, July 8, 1879, p. 45.
32. **Thirty-Four,** Wednesday, March 5, 1879, p. 2.

33. 1880 census, Tascosa, Oldham County, #2631 and #1518.
34. **Charles Goodnight — Cowman and Plainsman,** by J. Evetts Haley, p. 335.
35. 1880 census report for Tascosa, Oldham County.
36. Bonney dominated those weaker than himself particularly if they were not armed. These men were of danger to himself and such acts only enhanced his reputation among his own men.
37. **Texas' Last Frontier, Fort Stockton & Trans Pecos 1861-1895,** by Clayton W. Williams. Also **Fort Davis, Texas,** by Scobee and **Western Gunfighters** by Ed Barthelomew. C.L. Nevill, Musquiz Canyon, to J.B. Jones, July 19, 1881.

CHAPTER 5
SIDE LIGHTS

Further insight into the inaccuracy of Ash Upson's statements is the statement that he made in Garrett's book that in April of 1879 William Bonney had returned to Fort Sumner in order to steal stock when he had been in the custody of the sheriff of Lincoln from March until July of 1879 while trying to save his own skin in the Chapman murder by turning in his former friends. The particulars are as follows.

There had been bad blood between Bonney and Jesse Evans. Bonney had agreed to come into Lincoln and meet with Jesse Evans to settle their differences once and for all. They met that night in Lincoln and the group consisted of Bonney, Tom O'Folliard, Jesse Evans, James J. Dolan and William Campbell. Campbell was reputed to be a close relative of Jesse and Frank James of Missouri.

That chilly February of 1879, attorney H.S. Chapman of Las Vegas arrived in Lincoln to handle legal matters pertaining to the death of Sue McSween's husband Alexander. Bonney was already in town and soon the little group was seen walking about the streets of Lincoln in fine spirits. Chapman had just come out of a nearby building where he had put a bread poultice on his face due to a severe attack of neuralgia when he had the misfortune to run into the little group. Chapman's association with Sue McSween made him an immediate target for Dolan and Evan's anger. They accosted him on the street and demanded to know where he was going. Chapman threw caution to the winds and boldly informed them that it was none of their business. Soon heated words were exchanged.

We will never know the exact sequence of affairs that night that led to Chapman's death and must therefore rely upon what little documentation that has been handed down. Campbell reported that Chapman was shot two times through the body.

Governor Wallace kept his promise to Bonney and requested of the District Attorney that all charges be dropped in return for his testimony against Dolan, Evans and Campbell. The District Attorney was controlled by the Dolan/Murphy faction and so refused the request. Bonney was a clever young man and his winning ways and charm had helped him to manipulate the governor and later, when captured at Stinking Springs and in fear of his own safety, he once again attempted play upon Wallace's emotions and begged Wallace to keep the promise he could not legally honor. Bonney made it appear that his predicament was the fault of the governor.

Bonney then languished not as a prisoner but as a guest of the Territory in a local store where he was free to move about and receive friends and gifts openly. He had complete freedom of the establishment and the cuffs, at his request, had been placed on so loosely that he was able to remove them at any time he desired. Wallace, upon witnessing the flow of liquor, cigars and pretty girls, was appalled. They even serenaded him with music. Bonney was a prisoner in name only.

The cuffs were but one of several conditions set forth by Bonney in return for turning state's evidence. This legend was carried over to the killing of Deputy James W. Bell when writers unfamiliar with their subject claimed Bonney again slipped the cuffs from "his slim wrists" in order to attack and kill Bell though he stood for more than an hour afterwards before the entire town with them still on while he tried vainly to remove them.

Though Wallace had kept his part of the bargain to the extent of his appointed powers, he could not get the charges against Bonney dismissed. Bonney remained in his temporary self-imposed paradise despite this temporary setback until Jesse Evans and William Campbell broke jail at nearby Fort Stanton. Bonney now feared for his own life as Evans and Campbell might be aware of his agreement with the governor. The frightened Bonney removed the cuffs for the final time and rode quietly out of Lincoln.

Campbell, Evans and Dolan had already been indicted for the murder of Chapman entirely on the promised evidence of William Bonney.[1] A recruit known only as "Texas Jack" was guarding Evans and Campbell and departed voluntarily with them.[2] Shortly afterwards a scouting party came across Evans, Campbell and "Texas Jack" in a camp in the mountains near Dowlin's Mill. "Texas Jack" was captured while Evans and Campbell made their escape.[3] Local newspapers then made the claim that Campbell was actually one of the James Brothers of Missouri.[4] Later reports stated Evans and Campbell had been hiding in one of John Slaughter's cow camps and when they left they "borrowed" some of his cattle and were presumably bound for Arizona.[5]

It is interesting that Bonney not only knew Jesse James but that Jesse asked him to join the James gang. Frank, Jesse and the Younger brothers sometimes visited the Texas Panhandle, Las Vegas and California. The Youngers sometimes stayed in Scyene in Dallas County, Texas, where they killed a deputy and another individual. The James boys stayed in Big Wichita Valley while visiting their sister Mrs. Allen Parmer.[6] Sometimes Frank and Jesse kept a herd of horses along a creek near Sterling, Texas.[7]

Many famous outlaws from other states were frequent visitors to

New Mexico. It was not unusual for them to ride vast distances in order to pull off a robbery, steal cattle or see the country. The evidence of this was the long trek from Missouri to Northfield, Minnesota, by the James boys, Daltons and Youngers. William Bonney himself often made long trips into the Panhandle and west Texas as well.

When Dr. Henry F. Hoyt departed Tascosa and William Bonney's unlikely friendship, he set up medical practice in Las Vegas, New Mexico, along the old Santa Fe Trail. He never dreamed that he would meet William Bonney again, but Bonney spent much time in Las Vegas and was well-known about town. When Bonney and Hoyt again met each other in late July of 1879, Hoyt took Bonney to the fabulous Montezuma Hotel at nearby Hot Springs.

A man named Winfield Scott Moore bought the Montezuma Hotel from its original owners and renamed it the Adobe Hotel although the original name persisted. Moore purchased the property and reopened it in 1879 with 16 eastern investors paying out $17,000 for a new bath house. Mr. Moore was a boyhood companion of Frank and Jesse James.

That night Bonney introduced Dr. Hoyt to a pleasant man named Mr. Howard and the men chatted amiably for some time. Afterwards Bonney asked Hoyt if he knew who Mr. Howard was and Hoyt replied that he did not. When Bonney informed him of the identity of his dinner companion Hoyt was aghast. Later Hoyt checked with relatives of Jesse James and discovered the man was indeed the famous outlaw. Jesse had come to Las Vegas seeking a place of retirement and was looking the town over. He even asked Bonney to join his gang but he refused. [8]

Indeed, there is documentation to support that claim that Jesse James did visit Las Vegas on at least two different occasions. The **Las Vegas Optic** newspaper recorded these two visits.

> Jesse James was a guest at the Hot Springs from July 28 to 29. Of course it was not generally known. [9]

> Jesse James stayed last night at St. Nicholas Hotel. [10]

Winfield Scott Moore also used his relationship with the Missouri outlaw to perpetrate jokes on the unwary. He once introduced Jesse James, under his alias, to a former governor of the Territory who was unaware of the subterfuge until later.

Las Vegas attracted other big names. John "Doc" Holliday was a frequent visitor to the town as well as to Santa Fe. He opened a dental office on Center Street (now Lincoln Avenue) and was an old cronie of J.J. Webb and went to visit him. At that moment Webb was in jail on a charge of murder. Holliday had a grudge against Charlie White and shot and wounded him. Holliday killed another man he didn't like and when a complaint was lodged against him he fled back to Dodge City. [11]

"Doc" Holliday was known to visit Santa Fe upon occasion and in his passing, in August of 1879, had two charges lodged against him for Carrying Deadly Weapons and another two for Keeping a Gaming Table. [12]

When Bonney was in Las Vegas he often stayed at Close & Pattersons in Old Town. Old Town was filled with saloons, brothels, cafes and gaming tables. When not busy relieving others of their cattle, Bonney was busy relieving people's money at cards. The docket book in San Miguel County shows charge 1005 against him for Keeping a Gaming Table. [13] He was charged under the name of The Kid alias Wm. Antrim. Charge 1185 was filed against him for The Larceny of Cattle. Charge 1200 charged William Bonney, William Wilson, Samuel Cook and Thomas Pickett for The Larceny of Horses. The Las Cruces **Thirty-Four** reported that Bonney was once jailed in Las Vegas. "'Kid' the reputed Lincoln County desperado is in jail in Las Vegas." [14]

Though the statement has been made too often that Major Lawrence Murphy was the major power of the opposition during the Lincoln county War it is not so. The papers had reported that he had retired in 1878 to live on his ranch and was there during most of the fighting. His partner, James J. Dolan, was the power in and around Lincoln during this period and also afterwards.

Major Murphy died in Santa Fe at St. Vincent's Hospital on Sunday, October 29, 1878, of cancer. According to the news report he was reported to be 47 years of age at the time of his death. [15] However, the 1870 census report for Lincoln County disclosed his age in 1870 as 53 years making him 61 years old at the time of death. The census report listed James Dolan at age 32 that year.

James J. Dolan died February 26, 1898, and was buried in the Fritz Cemetery 9 miles east of Lincoln. The date of his birth is given as May 2, 1848. His wife Caroline F. Dolan is buried there also, having departed on September 29, 1886. His young son, Emil, died June 4, 1882, at the age of 2 years, 1 month and 2 days. Dolan's daughter Louise died February 9, 1889. Her birth date is recorded as November 30, 1883. [16]

Sheriff William Brady is buried near his ranch while his wife and son Robert are buried in nearby San Patricio Cemetery. [17] No middle name or initial has ever been known for Sheriff Brady and none appears on his birth certificate in Ireland.

Although Charlie Siringo had one previous run-in with William Bonney in December of 1880 he had a second, unexpected one in April, May or June of 1881. Siringo was attending a dance in Fort Sumner and began to cast lustful glances at Charlie Bowdre's widow. When the dance was over Siringo went to widow Bowdre's room and knocked on the door. Mrs. Bowdre opened the door but would not allow Siringo inside.

The reason was that she was sleeping that night with William Bonney and he was, at that very moment, inside the building listening to their conversation.[18]

Apparently Charlie Siringo must have enjoyed the New Mexico atmosphere for he purchased two separate parcels of land in Santa Fe in 1896 and one in 1914. On September 20, 1896, he purchased property from Charles Leon Allison and again on December 10th from Mr. Allison. Both purchases were located on the north road to Cerrillos. On August 31, 1914, Siringo returned to buy 50 acres of land from Mr. Allison.[19]

William Bonney had many mistresses and girlfriends in his brief lifetime. He fathered several children around Lincoln and Fort Sumner. Most of the women involved have refused to discuss the matter over the years but in Lincoln and Fort Sumner there were two women everyone discussed. Bonney had a girlfriend in Lincoln named Juana Montoya Patron. She belonged to the affluent Juan Patron family of Lincoln but led such an immoral life that the family ordered her to cease using their family name so she simply became known as Juana Montoya. Her nickname was **La Tullida** due to having a crippled arm.

In the 1880 census she gave her age as 23 years and had an illegitimate son named Alexander, apparently in honor of Alexander McSween. It is said that she took in wash for a living and her relationship with Bonney had not been surpressed over the years. A search of the marriage records for the following 15 years shows she never married in Lincoln. One writer claimed her son was named Ramon and later murdered a woman and was sentenced to the State Penitentiary in Santa Fe where he died. A search of penitentiary records by the warden failed to disclose anyone named Ramon or Montoya as having been or died there.[20]

Alexander was born in the year 1879 which would make his conception in 1878 when Bonney was living in Lincoln. Juana listed herself in the column reserved for single women, widows and divorcees. She could neither read nor write.

We do know that Bonney had several favorite women in the Fort Sumner area, Paulita Maxwell, Charlie Bowdre's widow and Nasaria Yerby. Abrana Garcia supposedly bore him a child but the most notable of these women was Nasaria Yerby.[21]

Nasaria Yerby was born in New Mexico in the year 1862. Both of her parents were native New Mexicans. She lived on the ranch of Tomas Yerby of Virginia where Charlie Bowdre worked and which was one of the favorite hideouts of William Bonney. Apparently she was the mistress of Tomas Yerby for they were not related to each other and it was the custom then for the mistress to take the name of her lover. In 1880 Nasaria had two children, both illegitimate, one possibly the son of Tomas Yerby. Juan was just 3 years old at this time but Florentina was only a year old making her conception date in 1879 when William Bonney was spending a lot of time in and around Fort Sumner. [22]

Many people in New Mexico have stated that Florentina never denied her outlaw parentage. Many other families have hidden Bonney's name in shame. Illegitimate births were looked upon with disgrace in the frontier days as William Bonney himself could attest.

History fails to record what happened to Nasaria Yerby but one writer professed that he had reason to believe that she had later moved to Las Vegas. A check of the Las Vegas City Directories from 1882 until 1932 does not disclose her name. [23] Two Yerbys are listed, however.

In 1896 a Juan Yerby appears as living at the E.H. Baca residence on Hot Springs Boulevard W.S. He gave his occupation as that of a barber. In 1906 he appears again on Pacific Street. The only other Yerby listing appears in 1919 for a Mrs. Matilda Yerby at 614 National Avenue. [24] A check was made of several of the funeral homes in hopes that Nasaria Yerby might have been buried by them but it proved to be fruitless. [25]

In the first week of May 1880 William Bonney and John Wilson rode into Albuquerque. There Bonney stole two horses and the men departed in the direction of Santa Fe. We do not know the facts surrounding the theft of the two horses but there is one unsupported version in the files of the Albuquerque City Library. As the story went a certain merchant located at the corner of First and Central had made slurring remarks as to Bonney's proficiency with a gun. Bonney and Wilson tied up their horses to some tamarisk trees where old Albuquerque High now stands. The merchant fled at their approach. Finding his quarry absent, Bonney then threw the merchant's plow and some merchandise into a ditch and departed with two of his horses. He then went north toward Santa Fe and here fiction ends and fact begins.

The theft was reported and Sheriff Perfecto Armijo formed a posse and took up the trail towards Santa Fe where they overtook Bonney and Wilson and a sharp fight ensued. Bonney and Wilson surrendered themselves and were returned to the Bernalillo County jail in Albuquerque. Though Bonney and Wilson were unharmed word quickly spread that he had been killed by the sheriff's posse. [26]

On May 7, 1880, William Bonney went to trial in Bernalillo County Court charged with causes 547 and 548 for Stealing a Horse. Wilson was charged with Larceny in causes 554 and 563 on May 8th. Bail was set at $500 for Bonney and $250 for Wilson but neither man could make bail so remained in jail. On May 11 Bonney entered a plea of guilty to both charges and was sentenced to five years incarceration in the Territorial Prison on cause 547. Cause 548 was then dismissed with the notation that upon his release from prison he was to be delivered to the Marshall of the Territory to stand trial for his other crimes.[27]

Charge 554 against Wilson was dropped under **nolle prosequi** (not prosecuted) and he was sentenced to serve five years in the Territorial Prison along with Bonney on charge 563. Both men were shackled together and returned to the Bernalillo County jail. None of the news accounts or court records refer to John Wilson as John B. "Squire" Wilson of Lincoln County fame. The 1880 census lists three John Wilsons.

The jail, a one-story adobe, was located in the southeast corner of the present day Old Town Plaza. The jail was easy to escape from and apparently prisoners did regularly. News accounts stated that an escape could be made with a simple piece of wire or a nail to unlock the shackles and locks. Both Wilson and Bonney escaped from the flimsy jail to add to its growing legend but their departure was due to outside assistance.

The same night they were jailed an angry crowd appeared before the jail demanding that Bonney be delivered into their hands for a lynching. The crowd was in a black mood and both Albuquerque and nearby Bernalillo were noted for their number of lynchings. Sheriff Armijo, to his credit, was able to talk them out of their intentions and dispersed the mob without further incident.[28]

With the crowd in an evil mood, Bonney was prompted to seek a safer climate, only this time it would be with the assistance of an unidentified person. Though both men were heavily shackled and in jail awaiting transfer to the Territorial prison, they were somehow placed unguarded one night in the outer jailroom where they were left alone the remainder of the night. It appears that bribery had also taken place. The jail had been the center of attention for some time by local newspapers and the sudden departure of its most famous inmate would only add fuel to the growing fire of criticism.

Whoever had smuggled tools and money to Bonney could not have done so without the cooperation of the jailers who were certainly low-paid. Included were files, a hacksaw and larger tools for digging through an adobe wall and both men spent hours sawing through their shackles and digging out through the wall. During this interlude not a single guard bothered to ascertain the source of the noise. Once freed of their heavy bonds they set about digging a hole through the adobe wall of the east side of the room at ground level. This also consumed an hour or so and created a considerable disturbance.

The newspaper lamented upon their escape. "Up the Spout, Salt Creek, or where the woodbine twineth is presumably the place to find them now, and if any of our legal authorities wish to indulge in a wild goose chase, the opportunity of pursuing the escaped jailbirds is a magnificent one."[29] The article expressed the sad conditions that prevailed in the jail that enabled any prisoner with so much as a piece of wire or a nail in his possession to escape. The editors bluntly stated that Bonney and Wilson had an outside benefactor.

The identity of this mysterious person will never be known but in the 1883 city directory Bonney's brother Joe was working in the Journal Hotel at the corner of Second and Silver streets and owned by Lawrence Marrian.[30] Joe had been in Albuquerque in 1881 in Old Town to meet Pat Garrett there and discuss the details of his brother's death. He does not appear in the 1880 census for Albuquerque but this does not mean he was not there for census reports often omit persons or entire families. There is one other possiblity, however.

Dr. Henry F. Hoyt had moved from Las Vegas to Bernalillo 18 miles north of Albuquerque. Hoyt stated in his book that after leaving Las Vegas he did not see Bonney again until March of 1881 when Tony Neis and Robert Olinger were taking him by train to Mesilla for trial in the Brady and Hindeman murders. Is it possible that his old friend, who was above suspicion, helped out a former companion?

Sheriff Armijo immediately wired all law officials between Albuquerque and Fort Sumner for it was certain that Bonney would return there. The only town informed to the south was Socorro but it was not felt that Bonney would flee in that direction. Again the experts were wrong.

Bonney was aware that the authorities would be expecting him to return to Fort Sumner so instead he went directly south through Socorro to Georgetown where he had lived as a boy. William Antrim was then living in Mogollon. Two weeks later, on June 6th, a census enumerator approached dwelling number 193 and knocked on the door. A boyish fellow with buck teeth answered the door and the enumerator quickly explained his mission. The young man stated that his name was William McCarty and gave his age as 21 years. To confuse anyone who might be on his trail he stated he had been born in Illinois and his parents were natives of Ireland. When asked is occupation Bonney must have had a trace of a smile on his face when he replied, "Dairyman."[31]

Listed next door was Bonney's former mentor (and his stepfather's former employer) Ed Moulton.

Bonney could not now stay long for the enumerator might have reported him so he departed (some say on a horse given him by Moulton, others say it was stolen) in the direction of Fort Sumner. He carefully approached it from the unguarded southern side.

His arrival in Fort Sumner was just in time to appear in the census report again for the Fort Sumner census was taken two weeks later than the Georgetown one. This time he gave his name as William Bonney and his marital status as single. He listed his profession as "working in cattle" and his age as 25 years. This time he claimed Missouri as his birthplace as well as that of his parents. [32] In the building next to his was his old friend and cohort, Charlie Bowdre.

NOTES
CHAPTER 5

1. **Thirty-Four,** March 19, 1879.
2. Ibid., April 9, 1879.
3. Ibid., April 16, 1879.
4. Ibid., May 14, 1879.
5. Ibid., May 28, 1879.
6. **History of Clay County and Northwest Texas,** by J.P. Earle.
7. State of Texas Historical marker in Sterling, Texas.
8. **Frontier Doctor,** by Dr. Henry F. Hoyt.
9. **Las Vegas Daily Optic,** December 2, 1879.
10. Ibid., April 17, 1880.
11. Ibid., December 12, 17, 18, 23, 1930.
12. Santa Fe Criminal Docket Books, 1879.
13. San Miguel County Criminal Docket Book. His name was later crossed off charges 1005 and 1185 due to his sudden departure.
14. **Thirty-Four,** September 24, 1879.
15. **Desperadoes of New Mexico,** by F. Stanley.
16. **New Mexico Cemetery Records,** by Mrs. Robert Irwin Corn.
17. Ibid.
18. **Riata and Spurs,** by Charlie Siringo.
19. Santa Fe County Real Estate Direct & Indirect Index to Deeds, Book A-D, 1848-1935.
20. Penitentiary of New Mexico records. Warden Harold A. Cox.
21. The correct spelling is Yerby and not Yerbe.
22. 1880 Census Report, Fort Sumner, New Mexico, p. 21, lines 40-42.
23. Las Vegas City Directories 1882-1932 conclusive.
24. Ibid.
25. Johnsen Memorial Mortuary in April 1984 and Gonzales Funeral Home in April 1984.
26. **Albuquerque Advance,** Saturday, May 8, 1880.
27. Bernalillo County Criminal Docket Book, pp. 268 & 269. May 7, 1880. Pages 270 & 271, May 7, 1880 (both men). Cost of case 547 was $18.37; case 548 $15.57; case 554 $10.05 and case 563 $12.05 from Cost Book.
28. Two years later Sheriff Armijo would again successfully turn away a lynch mob that desired Constable Milton J. Yarbery, a two-time murderer.
29. **Albuquerque Review,** May 20, 1880.
30. Albuquerque City Directory 1883.
31. 1880 census report, June 7, 1880, Georgetown, Grant County, House 193.
32. 1880 census report, June 17-19, 1880, Fort Sumner & Cedar Springs, San Miguel County, p. 436. The census shows John B. Wilson in Lincoln, John Wilson of White Oaks and John Wilson, Bonney's neighbor in Georgetown.

Purported photograph of Henry McCarty, later to become Billy the Kid. Probably taken in New York as estimated age here would be 10-11 years.

New York City in 1850. William Bonney lived within the circled area of lower east side Manhattan. Pearl and Vandewater streets (where he lived and committed the famous stabbing) lie in the center of the circle

Silver City, New Mexico,
in later years (circa 1915). It was
here Henry McCarty spent 2
years of his youthful life and
escaped jail to become an outlaw.

Mogollon, New Mexico, about 1910-11.
Left to right: Maurice E. Coates,
William "Uncle Bill" Antrim, Billy Clark.

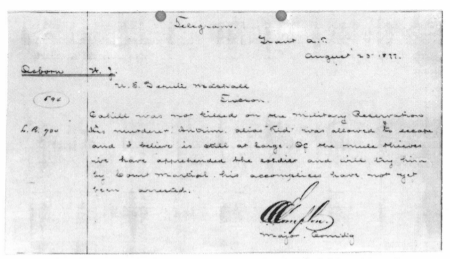

Copy of telegram concerning Billy's killing of civilian Frank P. Cahill from Major Compton, commanding officer of Camp Grant, Arizona, to U.S. Deputy Marshall W.J. Osborne. This is the first time the name "Kid" appears in documentation and prior to the time suggested by writers that he received the name.

Blazer's Mill ruins where Andrew "Buckshot" Roberts was killed by the Regulators.

Fort Sumner in the 1870's.

Original army map of Fort Sumner made July 1, 1868, showing layout of buildings and cemetery.

Wortley Hotel where Robert Olinger was feeding the prisoners when William Bonney shot Deputy J.W. Bell.

Pat Garrett

Billy LeRoy (right) the original Billy the Kid. His brother Sam is on the left the morning after their lynching in Del Norte, Colorado. Note the wire about their necks and legs and the cloth bandage for LeRoy's bullet would in the left calf.

William "Kid" Wilson, cohort of Henry Starr, the nephew of Belle Starr. Committed a robbery in Arkansas and arrested in Colorado Springs.

Another counterfeit Kid. William Cornelius, known as Billy the Kid, in Trinidad, Colorado, about 1888.

CHAPTER 6
FINAL DAYS

William Bonney always promoted himself whenever the opportunity presented itself. This was never more evident than after his capture at Stinking Springs and temporary incarceration at Las Vegas. During the seige of the house at Stinking Springs it was not William Bonney who ventured out the front door to converse with Pat Garrett and his men. It was Dave Rudabaugh. But once safely in Las Vegas when **Optic** reporter, George Fitzpatrick, came to interview the celebrated outlaws Bonney rushed forth to speak to him while Rudabaugh and the others refused to be interviewed.

The reporter was so smitten by Bonney's personality and outgoing charm that he unknowingly created a legend that day. He stated, "Bonney was the attraction of the show and one would scarcely mistrust that he was the hero of the 'Forty Thieves' romance which this paper has been running in serial form for six weeks or more. . . he looked and acted like a mere boy . . . looking like a schoolboy . . . he has agreeable and winning ways." [1] Fitzpatrick had fallen under the Bonney spell as had so many people before him and in doing so glorified a cowardly, petty outlaw into a historical legend.

Fitzpatrick also created another illusion that has remained for over a hundred years. At that time Bonney had only killed 3 men in his entire life so Fitzpatrick decided to embellish his own article with further glorification. Though Bonney never made such a statement, before or after the meeting, Fitzpatrick made up the byline that William H. Bonney had killed 21 men — one for each year of his life. Though untrue, Fitzpatrick had the only opportunity to interview the most famous outlaw in the Territory and he was out to make the best of it.

Bonney and company were delivered to the Santa Fe jail at seven-thirty in the evening and placed under the care of jailer Jose D. Silva. The following morning at eleven o'clock Pat Garrett arrived to inspect his prisoners and Bonney complained that he was hungry and had not been fed. Garrett checked the restaurant across the street that had the county contract for feeding of county prisoners and discovered that food had been sent to Bonney the previous night and that morning. In fact, jailer Silva had accepted the food on both occasions. Silva was confronted and admitted to having sold some of the food and eaten the rest.

A quick look at the census report and it is easy to understand why Silva needed the money as well as the food. He was 38 years old and had seven children ranging in age from six months to twenty-one years and jailers did not earn much of a salary. There were no further repetitions of such incidents after Garrett finished with Silva.[2]

While in Santa Fe Garrett ordered special shackles to be constructed and placed on Bonney. They were not of the conventional type because Garrett was well aware of his charge's ability to escape from jails and tight situations. They were constructed of the hardest metal known at the time and weighed a total of 15 pounds. They were not bolted or braded together but fused single piece much like a modern welding seam. Both ankles were shackled together by a short chain that did not allow Bonney to take a normal step (neither could he run) and chains ran to a belt at his waist. The shackles about the wrists were short also and likewise chained to the waist. Bonney could shuffle when he walked but could neither walk nor run. This becomes an important fact during his escape from the Lincoln County courthouse where some writers claimed Bonney ran ahead of Deputy J.W. Bell up the stairs. Bonney was wearing these shackles at the time.[3]

While in Santa Fe Bonney was placed alone in a cell without windows or furnishings of any sort. He sat in the center of the cell on a stool and was chained to the floor.[4] Most of the cells could be watched through an opening in the ceiling. Bonney's lack of accomodations would later become important.*

The two men selected to return Bonney to Mesilla for trial for the murders of "Buckshot" Roberts, William Brady and George Hindeman were Robert Olinger and Tony Neis. Olinger and Neis were huge men, each weighing in the neighborhood of 240 pounds. While in Santa Fe the newspapers reported that the two men had gone to a photography gallery to have their photo taken.

> Tony Neis and Bob Olinger, the twin deputies, have just had a photograph taken of themselves at Bennet & Brown's gallery. The picture is a good one and shows the two men off to advantage. They are both well grown boys, weighing perhaps 240 each, and are, what might be called, a heavy team. Bob had to sit down to keep his head in range of the camera.[5]

Tony Neis was of French descent and Robert Olinger a man with several cold-blooded murders to his account at Seven Rivers. While a deputy there he murdered one man by shaking his hand and pulling him forward while he shot him. In another instance he killed an innocent man for a friend.

John A. Jones went into partnership with John Beckwith in the cattle business but Beckwith tricked him by registering the joint brand in his name only, infuriating Jones. Jones threatened to kill Beckwith and told

*See Chapter 7 entitled "The Counterfeit Kids."

Milo Pierce he intended to do so. On August 29, 1879, Jones started in to give himself up to the authorities for fatally shooting Beckwith three days earlier. He rode up to Milo Pierce's rock house in Pierce Canyon. Pierce was sitting on a couch with Olinger when he saw Jones approaching.

Pierce then turned to Robert Olinger and remarked that he felt that Jones was coming to kill him and he didn't know what to do. Icily Olinger remarked, "I'll do it. Just sit still." Olinger reached for his rifle as Jones came in the door and the first shot accidentally hit Pierce in the hip. The second shot killed Jones. Governor Wallace reported to the Secretary of the Interior Carl Schurz that, "One 'Jim Beckwith' was shot and killed by one 'Tom Jones' and that 'Jones' was then killed by one 'Olinger,' to which, as the three are amongst the most bloody of the 'Bandits of the Pecos,' all the good people cried, 'Amen'."[6] This is why Pat Garrett often called red-haired Robert Olinger his "killer deputy."

Neis and Olinger loaded Bonney on the southbound train for Mesilla and made their first stop at Bernalillo. Dr. Hoyt happened to be standing on the platform, having moved to Bernalillo, when the train pulled in. Hoyt was bidding some friends goodby when he glanced up and saw Bonney's face at the window so he climbed aboard to speak to him. He was surprised to see his old friend seated by the window with two exceptionally large men beside him.

Hoyt inquired whether there was anything he could do for Bonney and Bonney smiled and replied that he would appreciate the use of Olinger's two pistols and shotgun for a few moments.

Olinger scowled and replied, "My boy, you had better tell your friend goodbye. Your days are short."[7]

Bonney laughed and replied, "Oh, I don't know. There's many a slip twixt the cup and the lip."[8] This was the second time Hoyt had heard Bonney utter this phrase and it was representative of what was to come.

Bonney was delivered to Mesilla to stand trial for three charges of murder. The "Buckshot" Roberts charge was dismissed due to the technicality that it occurred on federal property and was therefore not under the jurisdiction of the District Court. No federal charges were ever filed against Bonney concerning this crime. He was found guilty of the murder of William Brady and taken to Lincoln County where he was condemned to hang.

While Garrett was out of town purchasing lumber to build the gallows Deputies Robert Olinger and James W. Bell were left in charge of Bonney and approximately 14 other prisoners. Olinger disliked Bonney and being a bully taunted Bonney constantly, hoping to spark Bonney into making a provocative move that would give Olinger legal cause to kill him. Bell, on the other hand, was a complete opposite of Olinger. He treated his prisoner with decency.

James W. Bell was a former Texas Ranger and at one time lived in Dallas. In the spring of 1879 he left Dallas in the company of O.W. Williams (an engineer), N.B. Laughlin (a Dallas attorney), N.W.W. Fish, G.W. Irving (two recent Harvard graduates), J.Wyeth and S.D. Myers and headed for Leadville, Colorado, because of the excellent mining opportunities presented there.

Bell never made it to Leadville for on the way they heard of the carbonate mines at Cerrillos, New Mexico, and decided to go there instead. Bell remained in Cerrillos the remainder of the summer of 1879 before pulling up stakes for Lincoln where he was appointed as a Deputy Sheriff to Pat Garrett.[9]

Contrary to popular belief, there were many eyewitnesses to Bonney's escape at Lincoln, or at least to most of it. Some have made the statement that Bonney obtained a pistol left in the outhouse and used it on Bell. This is untrue. Pat Garrett located this pistol shortly after the escape. Bonney had been unaware of its existence. There was no way to inform him of its location for he was not allowed visitors. Someone friendly simply hid the gun in hopes that Bonney would discover the weapon but he never did. Garrett located it afterwards.

Olinger took the 14 prisoners a block down the street to the Wortley Hotel, leaving Bell alone with Bonney. It will never be known what occurred next but playing cards were scattered over the floor and Bell's head was cut from being struck. Bonney got Bell's pistol during the struggle and Bell fled out the door and down the stairs pursued by a Bonney that could not match his stride. Bonney hit the south wall with his shoulder and fired. The lead ball missed Bell and struck the lower wall beyond. The second hasty shot gouged a deep furrow in the adobe plaster along the north wall of the stairs and ricocheted into Bell's left side. Bell stumbled out the rear door and collapsed in the arms of Godfrey Gauss.

Bonney then threw his weight against the armory door only feet distant, bursting the frame and within moments had Olinger's shotgun with two loaded barrels. He returned to the northeast window where he had an unobstructed view of the approaching Olinger. One witness, reported in **Newman's Semi-Weekly,** was walking past the courthouse with Bob Ellis and had just reached La Rue's store when they heard firing.[10] Moments later Olinger rushed down the street, without prisoners, and turned into the gate directly beneath the northeast window where he heard Gauss's tale of Bell's death.

Gauss explained that Bell had staggered out the back door and then collapsed in his arms and that Bonney was armed and inside the building. As he finished this statement Olinger heard the words, "Hello, Bob!" Olinger then received two blasts of buckshot directly into the upper body and shoulders. He fell almost into the doorway that served as the town post office. Ellis and his companion saw smoke drifting from the building and at first thought some Mexicans were shooting up the town so paid it little heed.

Bonney then appeared on the small front porch located on the front of the second story. The porch was short and from this vantage he could not see Olinger's body. As a crowd gathered Bonney broke open the shotgun (the term "broke-open" in reference to a double-barrelled shotgun means to open the breech to extract or load the shells). He did not "break" the shotgun to pieces against the railing for it was still in existence years afterward. Neither could he throw down the pieces on Olinger's body as it was more than 60 feet distant around the corner. He returned the shotgun to the armory and picked up pistols and a rifle before returning to the porch. [11]

Bonney announced to the gathered audience that he held the town and all that were in it. He now had an arsenal composed of eight rifles and pistols. He ordered Godfrey Gauss to obtain tools to free him from his shackles. Both hands and feet at this time were still securely shackled eliminating the story that he had slipped off his cuffs. A pick was produced and Gauss worked on the chains for an hour and only successfully freed the left leg. Now Bonney could ride a horse but when he attempted to mount it threw him. Remounting he galloped westward to Ygenio Salazar's house with the eight weapons.

In early May the **Las Vegas Daily Optic** reported erroneously that a rumor had been relayed to them that Marshall Dallas Stoudenmire of El Paso, Texas, had shot and killed William Bonney but it had yet to be confirmed. It later proved to be an unfounded rumor for Bonney never went to El Paso following his escape from the Lincoln County courthouse. The editors expressed disbelief at the report for they felt Bonney was too shrewd to walk into the arms of the law in El Paso as the officers would have arrested him on sight. Actually they would not. There were no charges pending against Bonney in El Paso according to the Criminal Docket Books and since he was not wanted in Texas there was no reason to arrest him.

Still in existence today is the red leather wallet carried by Olinger at the moment of death. The wallet has dark stains formed by his dried blood and inside are six pieces of correspondence never before printed. The first is a letter written by Olinger in his own hand concerning the first time he was ever arrested.

The first time I was in jail March the 11th 1881 Arrested by order of L. Bradford, Prince Chief Justice of the Superior court of the first judicial district. Court charged with being a Deputy US Marshall and carrying Deadly weapons disarmed and sent to Jail after was Discharged from custody and allowed to carry arms.

A receipt from attorney A.J. Fountain in regards to the prosecution of a murder case Olinger was involved in.

Recd of Robt Ollinger Twenty five dollars as retainer fee to assist in prosecution of Marion Turner charged with murder.

A.J. Fountain
Atty at Large

There are two letters concerning the appointment of Robert Olinger as a U.S. Deputy Marshall and his own letter accepting same.

Robert Ollinger Esq   Mesilla NM. April 3/1880

Dear Sir;

Upon my recommendation the United States Marshall has appointed you his deputy in Lincoln County. I hope you will accept this appointment, and in that event suggest that you signify to the marshall your acceptance at your earliest convenience.

He well then send you papers for service.

Very respectfully
A.J. Fountain
I enclose appointment herewith
F.

Territory of New Mex
County Dona Ana

To all whom it may concern

Be it known that I have this day appointed Robert Olinger a Debuty Sheriff on an for the County of Dona Ana. And he is hereby charged with the Special trust of taking William Bony alias The Kid alias Henry Antrim from the County seat of Dona Ana Co. and Delivering him to the Sheriff of Lincoln County. With full powers and authority to summons Possy or to do any and all things necissary for the safe Delivery of Said Prisner in the hands of the above named Authinty.

Jas W. Fourtino
Sheriff

Mesilla N Mx
April 15th 1881

Territory of New Mex
County Dona Ana

I Robert Olinger having been duly appointed a Debuty Sheriff of the County of Dona Ana in said Territory do solemly swear that I will support the Constitution of the United States the Laws of the Territory of New Mexico and that I will faithfully and imparcially and to the best of my abillity discharge all the duties of said Debuty Sheriff writin and for said County during my witness in said office so help me God.

Robert Olinger

Subscribed and sworn before me this 15th day of April A.D. 1881.

George R. Bowman
Clerk Dist Court

There is an interesting letter from Joseph C. Lea concerning money Olinger deposited with him in order to purchase some land.

Roswell NM
Mch 31 st/81

Robt Olinger

Dear Sir;

Since getting your letter concluded not to send your money as you might not get it before leaving. But shall you need it, to buy the land you wanted, you can just draw on me to the amount of 300\frac{00}{100}$ as you have nearly that amt in my hands.

Yours in haste
J.C. Lea

This final bit of correspondence is the warrant signed by U.S. Marshall John Sherman concerning William Bonney, Doc Scurlock and others.

Office of the United States Marshal
Territory of New Mexico
Santa Fe, Apl 5th, 1880

Robert Ollinger Esq
 U.S. Deputy Marshal
 Roswell, NM

Dear Sir:

I sent you this day in a separate envelope Warrants against "Kid" Antrim alias Wm. Bony. Scurlock, et, al, also subponeas for Tittolman et, al. Please serve the subpoenas at once and tell the parties to be over here before the 12th or 14th (illegible) to testify in the case of the US vs Hawkins — the warrants you can execute where convenient — only they are returnable the 1st Monday in September next.

Very respectfully
John Sherman Jr.
US Marshal

Like a moth drawn ever constantly to the hot flame Bonney returned once more to his old haunts around Fort Sumner. His former companions had fled the territory long ago, leaving only him to face charges for a murder he was involved in but did not commit. He felt secure around Fort Sumner for he had many friends there and there were lots of pretty women. He stayed in the sheep and cow camps of everyone, including those of Pete Maxwell who was aware of this fact.

Shortly after the escape Barney Mason told the **Optic** that Bonney was staying in a cow camp near Consios Springs when Jim Currington chanced to ride unexpectedly upon him as he slept on the ground.[12] Currington was searching for some of his cattle and the frightened Bonney awakened at his approach and suddenly jumped upright. His quick movement startled his stolen horse which then broke away and ran off.

Mason reported that after escaping from Lincoln, Bonney went to the area of **Agua Azul** where he lost the horse stolen at the courthouse. During the night it returned only to break away from him once more when he attempted to saddle it. He walked to Newcomb's cow camp where he stole another horse from one of Newcomb's men and rode to the Currington range where Jim Currington chanced upon him.

Currington did not approach Bonney but gave him wide berth. Bonney was then forced to walk twelve miles to Buffalo Arroyo where he stole a fresh mount and made it into Fort Sumner by the west side of the Pecos River. He camped above town that night.

When Mason came in that Saturday night a man named Bell informed him that someone had stolen one of his horses and that he suspected the culprit was a Mexican. Mason and Jim Currington then rode up to Buffalo Arroyo looking for the animal when they suddenly came upon a sheep camp and recognized their horse. At their approach a man lying between some blankets bolted upright and it proved to be William Bonney. He was in the company of four Mexicans and the five men took positions as if to fight. Finally one Mexican rode out to Mason and informed him that Bonney was in their camp but that none of them were armed.

Mason and Currington were likewise not armed and they deemed it unwise to press their advantage so turned and rode for assistance, thus allowing Bonney the opportunity to escape once again.[13]

This was a few weeks following the escape from the Lincoln County courthouse when Bonney was in possession of eight weapons. Now he had none. The question arises as to what he did with them. His constant lack of a horse does little to enhance his reputation as a cattle thief. His constant loss of mounts occured on more than one occasion.

One instance was in 1879 or 1880 when he returned to the Silver City area while on his way to see brother Joe at Georgetown. He stopped by the home of Mary Richards Casey to pay his respects. He claimed he had shot an Indian along the Mimbres river in order to obtain his horse for his had run off. Whether this story was true or not, it may have been concocted to pacify Mary Richards Casey as to why he was riding a horse with a local brand. He asked to be fed and then asked to borrow money as he was broke. Mrs. Casey gave him what money she had and Bonney left. She never saw him again.

A month after Bonney's death an article appeared in the **Laredo Times** that has caused some confusion over the years. According to the article Bonney had ridden up to one of John Chisum's cow camps near Roswell and shot down three cowboys without warning. He allowed the fourth to return to John Chisum with the warning that this was just the beginning. He would continue killing Chisum cowhands until Chisum's $500 debt to him was satisfied. [14] There are no criminal charges in the docket books relating to this mysterious occurrence and no one in New Mexico ever knew anything about it. As it later turned out it was just another bit of yellow journalism created by a reporter on a slow news day.

The bit of misinformation first appeared in the **Las Vegas Daily Optic** on June 10th from a rumor passed on by some unidentified source. [15] The **Optic** printed a rumor without checking on its authenticity and the **Laredo Times,** also on a slow day, picked up the item as a filler. On June 16th the **Morning Gazette** of Las Vegas retracted the story and branded it as false and without foundation. [16] Unfortunately the **Laredo Times** felt no such responsibility toward its readers.

Bonney's final act of murder was just as heinous and brutal as his first but far more cowardly. A man named Joe Grant was in the Bob Hargrove saloon in Fort Sumner drinking heavily and boasting that he would kill William Bonney on sight. Grant and Bonney did not know each other and Joe Grant had not made the decision on his own. Grant was a close companion of John Chisum's cousin Finian Chisum and it was suspected that John Chisum or one of his relatives had paid Grant to get rid of Bonney.

Grant's threats and daily activities had been reported to Bonney who remained in seclusion and far away from town. When the time was ripe Bonney and a friend rode into Fort Sumner. It was January 10, 1880.

Grant had held court in the Bob Hargrove saloon for days while Bonney continued receiving reports on Grant's activities and the amount of liquor he was consuming. Bonney rode directly to the Hargrove saloon and before entering he turned to his companion and said, "I bet I kill a man today before you do." [17] Bonney was aware that Grant had been drinking for days and by now was in a state of drunkeness. It was time for Bonney to make his move.

Bonney walked into the saloon and ordered a drink from Jesus Silva. He remained standing at the bar. As Silva poured the liquor Grant began to berate and antagonize Bonney from across the room but by now Grant was in no condition to be walking such a fine line between life and death. Finian Chisum stood at Grant's elbow and witnesses later related that Finian Chisum and Grant had exchanged pistols as soon as Bonney walked into the room.

Bonney knew that Grant was now too inebriated to be of any danger so he ignored the insults and taunts and pretended to admire the ivory-handled six gun Grant had at his waist. Bonney then inquired as to whether he might have a look at such a fancy weapon and Grant walked up to the bar and handed him the gun. He was so drunk now he could not see the danger in it and it cost him his life. As Bonney later related to Pat Garrett and others, he had spun the cylinder in order to determine whether he might be able to slip a few rounds out of it and thus insure himself against possible harm.

In this admission Bonney was saying that his actions were premeditated and that he did not intend it to be a fair fight. The chips would, as always, be stacked in Bonney's favor before he would commit himself to any action. He was setting Joe Grant up for the slaughter.

Bonney was surprised, and delighted, to discover that Grant had three empty chambers in his pistol so Bonney spun the cylinder until the hammer rested on the third cartridge. The next three times the gun was cocked and the trigger pulled the hammer would fall harmlessly on empty chambers. With this advantage now taken care of Bonney knew Grant was as good as dead. He returned the pistol to Grant and now became very brave in his own actions and began to return Grant's insults.

Bonney was not much of a drinker in New Mexico and no one had ever seen him in a state of intoxication for he certainly needed his wits about him at all times. He never made the mistake Joe Grant was making. He toyed with his drink but never raised it from the bar as he waited for Grant to make the move he knew must now come. When Grant's temper reached the flash point he drew his pistol, pointed it at Bonney's midsection, cocked it and pulled the trigger. There was no explosion of black powder. No deafening sound -- only the chilling metallic click.

Bonney was in no hurry to perform the **coup de grace** and slowly removed his gun from its holster and thumbed back the hammer. Grant's second try was no better than the first and again met with failure. Before Grant could try the third time Bonney placed the muzzle of his pistol in Grant's face and pulled the trigger. Two hundred and fifty grains of soft lead backed by forty grains of black powder suddenly came to life in a flash of flame and smoke as the ball plowed into Grant's forehead killing him instantly.

Before the room had cleared of smoke Billy walked over to the lifeless corpse, emptied the pockets of money, stepped back to the bar where he paid his bill with the dead man's money, downed the drink and walked out the door.[18]

It was to be his final murder. The next time around Lady Luck would abandon him and it would become William Bonney's turn. His time was swiftly running out.

Time finally ceased on the night of July 14, 1881. Pat Garrett knew more about Bonney's whereabouts than he ever admitted publicly. Garrett had many loyal friends in Fort Sumner, including Barney Mason, and since Mason had been giving the newspapers descriptions of Bonney's whereabouts following the escape it was certain that he was also telling Garrett. Reports were coming in to him from time to time concerning Bonney in the Fort Sumner area. When the time was ripe Garrett felt it was time to shut the gate.

Garrett sought out John W. Poe, former deputy in Mobeetie, Texas, and Thomas K. "Kip" Kinney to assist him. He informed them of his plans and wrote to Joseph C. Lea of Roswell of his proposed intentions. That night the men went up the Pecos to meet Wayne Brazil.

Brazil had been dodging Bonney around Fort Sumner since the escape for fear of his own safety. Brazil had made known to Pat Garrett that he had heard Bonney was still in the Fort Sumner vicinity though he had not seen him personally. Garrett had written Brazil and told him to meet them at the mouth of Arroyo Taiban (Stinking Springs) on the night of July 13 to discuss their mutual problem.

There were others that kept Garrett informed. After Bonney's death many remained silent of their possible participation in order to protect themselves from possible harm from Bonney's friends. Most notable would be Barney Mason, Sabinal Gutierrez and Pete Maxwell.

The party crossed Salt Creek flowing out of the Capitan Mountains and past Bosque Grande where the river widened to three miles in width. Gamma grass was thick here; sometimes as high as three feet. From there to Fort Sumner the river was barren and unfriendly. They traveled mostly at night and remained a half-mile off the trail in order not to be recognized and arrived at the mouth of the Taiban Arroyo an hour after dark. Brazil was not in evidence and after a two hour wait Brazil still had not put in an appearance. He was too frightened for his life.

They made camp a mile or so away that night and the following morning they scoured the countryside with field glasses for signs of Brazil but he was not forthcoming. They saw nothing that roused their suspicions.

Since John Poe was unknown in Fort Sumner, Garrett selected him to ride into the old military post to see what information he might discover. Poe also rode to Sunnyside (now present day Fort Sumner) seven miles above the post to see Milnor Rudolph who was a good friend of Pat Garrett. He returned after sundown with nothing of value to report.

Rudolph told Poe that all indications pointed to Bonney's presence in the area but he did not know where. Bonney had numerous girl friends in the vicinity and was staying at various cattle and sheep camps including those of Pete Maxwell. In the back of Garrett's mind must have been Paulita Maxwell and Bonney's relationship with her. Bonney was no fool, but still . . . when it came to women. . .

That night they headed into Fort Sumner. The most important fact here is that when Garrett went into town that night he did not do so to scout around. Instead he went directly, and without hesitation, to one person and one person only, Pete Maxwell. Old-timers of Fort Sumner have often stated over the years that Pete Maxwell had a lot more to do with Bonney's death than has ever seen print.

They tied their horses up in a grove in the camp of a man named Jacob and enjoyed a cup of coffee with him before pressing on. They moved swiftly, but cautiously, through the darkness and entered Fort Sumner through a cluster of adobe buildings.

Nearing the Maxwell residence they spotted a group of Mexicans squatting around a fire and talking, unaware of the presence of the three intruders. Garrett took them to be laborers of the Maxwell family. As they watched one man stood up, bid his companions good night in Spanish and walked off toward the old military barracks fronting the parade ground. He wore a broad-rimmed hat, dark vest, long-sleeved white shirt and a beard.

Garrett's first opportunity to catch William Bonney had just unknowingly slipped through his hands. The man was indeed William Bonney who had grown a beard in order to foil recognition. His fluent Spanish had completely fooled Garrett. Bonney strolled into one of the small adobe rooms occupied by Celsa Gutierrez.

Celsa Gutierrez was related to Pat Garrett by his first marriage for she was the sister of his first wife who later died. Celsa was married to Sabinal Gutierrez and her intimate relationship with Bonney would have given Sabinal cause enough to keep Garrett or Pete Maxwell informed of the whereabouts of Bonney.

When Bonney entered the room he was sharing with Celsa he removed his gunbelt, boots and hat. He lay down on the bed to relax and read an old newspaper. He thumbed through the pages and called out to Celsa that he was hungry and wanted something to eat. Celsa replied that she had nothing but if Bonney wanted some meat Senor Pete had a side of beef hanging on the porch and if Bonney were willing enough to fetch it she would cook it for him. Bonney picked up a small butcher knife and strolled down the side of the parade grounds minus his boots, gun and hat. He was not expecting any trouble that night.

Meanwhile, Garrett and his deputies were already at the Maxwell residence. Poe and Kinney remained on the porch while Garrett went inside to speak to Maxwell. Garrett's desire to speak to Maxwell alone is an indication that he did not wish to reveal Pete Maxwell's part in locating Bonney. If anyone should know, Maxwell would for he employed more men in the area than any other individual and he knew that Bonney was staying in his cow and sheep camps from time to time. Then there was the matter of Paulita . . .

Pete Maxwell's room was located on the southeast corner of the old officer's quarters facing the parade ground. Celsa's room was in the long building next to his. The only door was located on the south side beside a window and a second window was in the wall on the east side facing the porch where Poe and Kinney sat. Along the west wall was a fireplace.

Garrett shook Maxwell who was sleeping and began speaking to him. The conversation that occurred between the two men must have taken longer than related later by Garrett for Bonney had to walk over 60 yards to the Maxwell residence. Garrett stated that in answer to his question concerning Bonney's whereabouts Maxwell replied that he didn't know. Bonney was sleeping with one of Maxwell's employees only a short distance away and the relationship was as well known to Maxwell and everyone else in Fort Sumner as it was to Sabinal Gutierrez.

Bonney turned north down the fence that ran in front of the Maxwell home and approached the porch, unaware of the two figures seated in the shadows of the porch. Poe was reclining in a chair while Kinney stood in the yard. Poe noticed the approach of a figure he took to be a Mexican laborer. Not wishing to have the man suddenly walk up on two strangers in the dark and become frightened Poe started to stand up and speak with the man when his spur caught in a crack in the porch, causing him to stumble.

The approaching figure heard the sound and froze. Bonney did not know the strangers nor their reason for being on Maxwell's porch but thinking they were Mexican he spoke to them in Spanish. "Quien es? Quien es?" he repeated, backing defensively toward Maxwell's open bedroom door. Poe attempted to speak to the man but the figure continued to retreat toward the door. Poe did not want the man to suddenly walk in on Garrett in the dark but there was nothing he could do.

Bonney stepped half-way into the door frame with his eyes frozen on the men outside. "Pete, who are those men outside?" he asked anxiously. Garrett's back was to the door and he suddenly recognized a familiar voice. For the moment all he knew was that William Bonney had ambushed him. Garrett half-turned in a crouch, drew his 7½ inch barrel Colt and fired a shot at the figure still inside the door frame. The shot caught Bonney in the left side of the breast and traversed through his heart. Garrett did not know Bonney was mortally hit and fired another shot. This one was wild and as Bonney went down the bullet passed harmlessly over him and struck a metal wash basin with a loud metallic clang.

Pandemonium broke out. As the explosion of the first shot lit up the tiny room the frightened Maxwell leaped out of bed and through the open door, vaulting over the still form on the floor. Garrett followed immediately shouting excitedly that he had just shot and killed William Bonney. Poe still felt Garrett had shot one of Maxwell's laborers by mistake.

There was no dishonor in what Pat Garrett did that night. He did exactly what he was paid to do and did it in fear of his own life. Garrett thought he had been ambushed and with a known killer standing behind him in the dark he did the very thing anyone would have done — defended himself.

People began to pour out of doorways of nearby buildings but no one would dare enter the darkened room for fear Bonney was only wounded and still armed. Up till that moment everyone, including Pat Garrett, thought Bonney had a pistol. It would be suicide for anyone to walk through that door.

Deluvina Maxwell fetched a lighted candle and placed it in the open window. Jesus Silva was in the crowd that night and volunteered to enter the room first. He was a close friend of Bonney and felt that no harm would come to him at Bonney's hands. He stuck his head inside the door and peered into the dimness. Soon he could make out the lifeless form of the young desperado lying on the floor, his feet in the doorway and his head facing the fireplace. Upon examination it was discovered that Bonney was bootless, hatless and without a pistol but he did have a weapon in his hand — a knife. His pistol, a .38 Colt double action Lightning, was found in Celsa Gutierrez's room. [19]

Henry McCarty had come a long way from the slums of New York City to die on the dirt floor of an adobe room. Henry McCarty alias Henry Antrim alias Kid alias William H. Bonney was dead and now the legend began.

Bonney's only shirt was bloodied with a small hole over the side of the left breast. It was removed and replaced with one of Pete Maxwell's shirts which was pinned in back in order to make it fit. The body was placed inside the church on a plank supported at each end by a large barrel. Lighted candles were placed at the foot and head. Deluvina finally locked the doors to keep people out and remained with the body the entire night.

The following morning the corpse was taken a mile and a half east to the old military graveyard and deposited beneath the earth forever. To this day no one knows just which grave is his or where it lies but a marker was erected for the thousands of tourists that come to Fort Sumner each year to visit the grave of the outlaw known as Billy the Kid.

NOTES
CHAPTER 6

1. **Las Vegas Gazette**, December 27, 1880.
2. June 1880 Census Report, Santa Fe County, New Mexico.
3. **Frontier Doctor**, by Dr. Henry F. Hoyt and an unknown dated issue of **The Santa Fe New Mexican**. The jail was located on Water Street.
4. See Chapter 7 entitled "The Counterfeit Kids."
5. **Daily New Mexican**, March 2, 1881.
6. **The English Westerner's Brand Book**, Vol. 5, No. 4, July 1963, Publication No. 90. Story of the Beckwiths & Olinger by Phil Rasch.
7. **Frontier Doctor**, by Dr. Henry F. Hoyt.
8. Ibid.
9. **Pioneer Surveyor-Frontier Lawyer**, by S.D. Myres.
10. **Newman's Semi-Weekly, Supplement to the New Southwest & Herald**, May 14, 1881.
11. Godfrey Gauss' Affidavit in the **Lincoln County Leader**, January 15, 1890. No eye-witness ever made the statement that Bonney shattered the shotgun against the railing or threw the pieces on Olinger's body.
12. **Las Vegas Daily Optic**, Monday, May 9, 1881.
13. **Las Vegas Morning Gazette**, Thursday, June 16, 1881.
14. **Laredo Times**, August 10, 1881.
15. **Las Vegas Daily Optic**, Friday, June 10, 1881.
16. **Las Vegas Morning Gazette**, Thursday, June 16, 1881.
17. Bartender Jesus Silva to his grandson C.G. Silva.
18. Ibid.
19. Poe stated that he never saw the pistol until Garrett returned with it from Celsa Gutierrez' room.

CHAPTER 7
COUNTERFEIT KIDS

Outlaws of the old west were known by many names and many aliases and were usually identified by a large number of sobriquets and nicknames. While some names were simply descriptions of the individual, all too often outlaws simply borrowed the aliases of others. There were many variations.

The most commonly-used form was that of "Kid" and was not only applicable to those of youthful appearance but quite often to adults as well. Sometimes the term Kid denoted age or origin and other times it appears to be only three letters in front of the individual's name.

The most famous case in point is that of Kid Curry, the Sundance Kid and Billy the Kid. One outlaw operating under a particular alias was often imitated by others in another location.

There were two Blackjacks (one Christian, one Ketchum), two William Currys, at least three William Bonneys, many Billy the Kids and so many Kid so-and-so's that you couldn't count them. While Henry McCarty was to become the most famous of the kids he certainly wasn't the first outlaw to use the name nor was he the last. He was simply a latecomer and therefore one of the counterfeit Kids.

There was James "Kid" Lewis, an Arizona fugitive being held in the Silver City jail in July of 1883 and later turned over to the sheriff of Graham County, Arizona.[1]

Nine years after Henry McCarty Antrim escaped from that same jail the sheriff's register of prisoners disclosed one William McCarty incarcerated there. He was born in New York City, brown haired, blue-eyed and a fair complexion. He was jailed for the crime of larceny.[2] He was released by the Grant County Commissioners on March 4, 1884, and under the heading of "Description" it stated that "he is a little cockeyed."

The "Catfish Kid" was one John B. Gough who was involved with other outlaws prior to his entry into Tascosa, Texas, where he was wounded in a shootout with a group of fellows and charged with murder, a charge which was later dismissed. On June 23, 1887, he wandered into a shed behind the Cone and Duran store where he engaged in conversation with two statecoach hands who were spending the night there. Their conversation angered another individual who was attempting to sleep (Pete Fulton) and he came toward the Catfish Kid with anger in his heart and was shot to death for his trouble.

The **Tascosa Pioneer** said that, "It was a cold-blooded murder and

Catfish Kid should be dealt with. He has done enough meanness around here already . . . A hempen lesson is all his case deserves. His kind should be thinned out as soon as possible.[3]

He was. The Catfish Kid was found guilty and sentenced to the penitentiary where he died a few years later.

In 1883 a young outlaw emulated William H. Bonney's short but sad career and took his name and hoped to make it famous. He was involved in only one known major crime in Stoneville, Montana. He survived a seige by lawmen in a deserted cabin and fled down the river bottom into obscurity and was supposedly never seen or heard from again.[4]

Some years later in Montana a Kid McCarty was hired on as a sheepherder to a local rancher. When he died the rancher claimed that the corpse was that of William "Kid" Bonney of the Stoneville fight but this has never been verified as so.

A few years following Bonney's death another Billy the Kid appeared in Las Vegas, New Mexico, along with another man known as The Pockmarked Kid. The identity of either man is not known.[5]

A petty outlaw named Kid Johnson operated around Gallup, New Mexico, in the late 1880's and in 1888 he murdered Marshall McGuire and a policeman, Henry, with the assistance of his partner Charlie Ross. Both men were tried and convicted of murder.

The lives of the Sundance Kid (Harry Longabaugh) and the two Kid Currys are so well documented that they do not deserve further reflection here.

Hank Winnie lived in Hot Springs (Now Truth or Consequences), New Mexico, in Sierra County where he was known locally as Billy the Kid. On November 11, 1890, he was charged with the crime of Assault With A Deadly Weapon but fled and was never apprehended.[6]

Colorado also had two Billy the Kids. One was William Cornelius who operated around Trinidad. He was arrested in Animas County for stealing some horses from David F. Barrett and a warrant for his arrest was issued in 1888.[7] The other Billy the Kid was the first to use that name and will be discussed in greater depth in a moment.

There was a William H. (Harrison) "Kid" Wilson involved in the famous Lincoln County War and was a companion of William H. Bonney. In a letter to Governor Lew Wallace Bonney referred to himself and Wilson as "the two Billies." Some confusion has resulted among some writers and historians concerning the two Billies who were the same size, shape and approximate age. The deeds of one have sometimes been attributed to the other.

There was a second William Wilson operating in Arkansas with Henry Starr, the celebrated nephew of the woman bandit known as Belle

Starr. In July of 1903 he was unceremoniously captured without a struggle in a Colorado Springs whorehouse with his pants down. He was 25 years of age at the time. Starr, Wilson and three other men robbed a bank at Bentonville, Arkansas, in June of that same year and escaped amid a hail of lead balls launched in their immediate direction. They escaped with $11,000 in cash but were apprehended the following month.

Billy the Kid of southeastern Arizona was one William F. Claiborne who became famous for a brief period of time during the Battle of the O.K. Corral in Tombstone which didn't actually occur at the corral at all but beside the photography studio of C.S. Fly. Though only a young boy at the time he stood beside Ike Clanton, Tom and Frank McLowery on October 26, 1881. Pitted against them were Wyatt, Virgil and Morgan Earp and John "Doc" Holliday. The **Tombstone Epitaph** of November 18, 1882, told of his death.

On a Tuesday morning around seven o'clock one Frank Leslie, better known as "Buckskin Frank," was in the Oriental saloon conversing with friends when Billy the Kid Claiborne pushed his way up to the group and began using abusive language. According to Leslie's account in which he deliberately played down his own part for he was a killer and murderer of many men, he politely told Billy the Kid, "Billy, don't interfere, those people are friends among themselves and are not talking about politics at all, and don't want you about." This would be a rather mild version for Leslie was given to strong profanity.

Leslie claimed he left Claiborne to join the group but Claiborne returned and began using abusive language again so Leslie took him by the scruff of the coat and led him away, all the while telling him not to get mad for if he persisted he might get into trouble. Claiborne shook Leslie loose, stuck his finger in Leslie's face and said, "That's all right, Leslie, I'll get even on you," and left the saloon. Shortly afterwards a man came in and informed Leslie that Claiborne was waiting outside to shoot him. Moments later a second informant also told him of Claiborne's presence.

Leslie stepped outside and saw the end of a rifle barrel protruding from behind a fruit stand and called out for Claiborne not to shoot. Before he had finished uttering this statement Claiborne fired his rifle, the bullet striking the sidewalk. Leslie aimed his pistol at Claiborne's breast and fired one shot which entered the left side of the breast and exited close to the spinal column. Claiborne made a few choice statements about Leslie's ancestry and then died.

There was a third Kid involved with William Bonney in Lincoln County and his name was G.H. "Kid" Dobbs. When Bonney and his crew arrived in Tascosa, Texas, in October of 1878 to sell stolen horses many of his men left him there and Dobbs was one of them. Dobbs went to work as a cowhand for one of the local ranchers in the Panhandle. Dobbs was later a member of a four man party sent out by Panhandle ranchers to kill Bonney and they trailed him into White Oaks where Bonney had sold his stolen Texas beeves to a local butcher.

El Paso claimed another kid to add to the growing list. "The 'Rangers' at El Paso on last Saturday arrested three men, accused of cattle stealing, and hold them prisoners. Their names are Collins alias Montana, Charlie ____, the man who stole the pistol from Williams, the pump man, last summer and a man called Kid."[8] No further information appeared in the paper concerning this arrest or the individuals and El Paso has long since thrown away tons of their old records, including the Criminal Docket Books, so identification is impossible. We will never know if Charlie was Charlie Bowdre and Kid was William Bonney.

The El Paso Criminal Docket register of the 1890's disclosed the name of one J. Elliott alias "The Kid." There is no further information on this person.

Even New York City proclaimed its own Kid in "Davey the Kid" who, in association with John Flynn, stole a diamond earring from an unidentified woman on Fifth Avenue. Davey the Kid was arrested and sentenced to eighteen months in the State Prison.[9]

On September 16, 1887, Kid Swingle, Billy Bonner, "Kentuck" O'Callon and two unidentified outlaws held up engine Number 7 of the Atlantic & Pacific Railroad near Navajo, Arizona. Two bandits were killed when the posse caught up with them and later O'Callon was killed at Allentown, New Mexico in a cafe resisting arrest. Bonner was killed by a posse out of Gila County, Arizona, and none of the stolen money was ever recovered nor found on the bodies. The loot ran from $38,000 to $75,000 depending on whether you believed the company express agents, the Wells Fargo investigator or the company employees.

Kid Swingle was recognized in Albuquerque but escaped into Texas before he could be apprehended. He was finally arrested in Joplin, Missouri. The November 19th issue of the Tucson **Arizona Star** said, "Kid Swingle escaped Sheriff Owens by jumping from a train window near Toyah, Texas." The Kid was never seen again and the money never recovered.[10]

The first, and original, Billy the Kid was known as Billy LeRoy although some said his real name was Arthur Pond or Potter. He operated in southern Colorado and northeastern New Mexico from 1876-1881 in conjunction with his brother Sam who sometimes went by the name of Silas Porter.

We know absolutely nothing about LeRoy's earlier life or where he was born. His early life was fabricated in print (as Upson did with Bonney) in a dime novel entitled **Billy LeRoy, the Colorado Bandit, Or, The King of the Highwaymen** which was almost the same title as the Bonney epic. It was published by Richard K. Fox and first appeared in the **Police Gazette.** Later rumors said LeRoy came from Indianapolis which was mixing LeRoy with Bonney who was mixed with William Antrim.

The book on Bonney was entitled **Billy the Kid, Or, The King of American Highwaymen.** This makes one wonder whether the same man authored both fantasies. Legend has it that one Thomas F. Dagett was the author of the LeRoy book.

Although LeRoy's early life is fictitious it is only given here as a piece of folklore Americana. LeRoy first got into trouble at the age of ten years and, like Bonney, was a juvenile delinquent. By eighteen he was arrested and confined in a second floor jail cell that he escaped from by jumping out of the window (no bars?) Up to this point the Bonney/LeRoy epics parallel each other.

LeRoy supposedly fled to a city the author identified only as H____ which was a stopping place for drovers somewhere between Chicago and New York. Here he robbed and killed a drover named John Hamer five miles outside of town.

LeRoy's next destination was the lusty town of Leadville, Colorado, where he alledgedly became a female impersonator. It must be injected here that a similar story has been made about Bonney in Silver City where he stole some women's clothes and went about town dressed up in them and was thus arrested. Another person claimed, years afterwards, that Bonney appeared in school plays at the Morrill Opera House dressed as a girl but none of his schoolmates or people that knew him then recalled such incidents.

LeRoy was billed as "Billy LeRoy, the greatest female impersonator of the age. This wonderful performer has been the delight and admiration of the leading cities of the U.S. and Europe." He shared the bill with a woman named May Vivian. "Dead Shot Charlie" also had his eye on Vivian and LeRoy finally shot him to death in a dispute over her attentions and fled Leadville. It is at this juncture that fantasy ends and fact begins.

We do not know the exact date of LeRoy's entry into southeastern Colorado but it is established that by 1874 he was already known as a coach and wagon robber along the heavily traveled trails.

In December of 1874 a Catholic nun named Sister Blandina arrived in Trinidad, Colorado. By that time LeRoy was a household name around Trinidad and his name was said to have appeared frequently in the newspapers concerning his depredations. He ran a small but tightly knit band of robbers and in personal appearance he and Bonney were the same height, hair and eye color, weight and general description. LeRoy was a year older than Bonney but like him he also appeared to be younger than his actual years.

Sister Blandina took charge of the small parochial school where she taught classes and engaged in medical work. In her book **At the End of the Santa Fe Trail** she stated she often heard the name of Billy the Kid around town as local citizens were afraid of him and news of his robberies were in the papers. One thing was certain — Sister Blandina led the cloistered, secluded life of a nun who was normally out of touch with the times and real world and had little time to spend on reading newspapers and keeping up with the events of the day. She was also lax in her use of words in her letters because she was not as aware of the passage of time as others. Most of her information came to her by word of mouth and then some time after it had occured. This has caused some confusion over the years.

Sister Blandina had never bothered to learn Billy the Kid's name although it must have been printed in the papers from time to time and spoken about town. She never knew him by any other name than Billy the Kid and it was not until she had been transferred to Santa Fe that she read the name of Billy the Kid involved in the Lincoln County War and thought it was the same person. When Bonney died in July of 1881 she wrote another nun and said that finally she had learned the name of her friend Billy the Kid, his name was William Bonney. LeRoy had been dead for two months but this was not reported in the Santa Fe papers.

In September of 1876 she was contacted by a member of the LeRoy gang to come to a certain place alone to give medical aid to one of the outlaws who had been wounded by Uncle Dick Wooten, the tollkeeper of Raton Pass. None of the local Trinidad doctors would administer to the outlaw identified only as "Happy Jack" and therefore the nun was summoned. Sister Blandina treated the wound, which was not a serious one, and was then asked whether she would like to meet the famous Billy the Kid. She replied that she would and she waited patiently in the cabin until Billy the Kid arrived.

At two o'clock that afternoon LeRoy rode up and was introduced to Sister Blandina only as Billy the Kid. He told her he was then on his way to Trinidad to murder all the doctors there for refusing to treat "Happy Jack's" wounds. Only by careful persuasion was the nun able to convince the young outlaw not to commit this deed for that would leave the town without medical aid of any sort. Surprisingly, he consented.

Sister Blandina described her Billy the Kid as having "steel-blue eyes, a peach complexion and was about seventeen years of age." She also said that he was well-mannered.

Though LeRoy kept his word concerning the doctors he made a raid upon the town instead and this was duly reported in the **Trinidad Enter-prise**. Not long afterwards LeRoy's brother Sam was captured and incarcerated in the Trinidad jail. A member of the Trinidad Vigilante Club escorted the nun to the jail to meet Sam whom the nun reported in her letters was a "partner" of Billy the Kid. Until the day she died she never realized this was LeRoy's brother or that she had mistaken Bonney for LeRoy.

In June of 1877 Sister Blandina was ordered to St. Vincent's Hospital and Asylum in Santa Fe. She was traveling with other nuns in a buggy with a driver and the Staab Brothers who later owned a store in Santa Fe. Billy the Kid had been raiding northeastern New Mexico heavily at that time and the countryside was in great excitement over where he might strike next.

According to Sister Blandina, somewhere outside of Sweetwater, the driver spotted a solitary rider approaching in the distance and his progress was duly noted by all. It proved be Billy the Kid and upon recognizing the nun in the carriage allowed them to pass unmolested while he gave them a demonstration of horsemanship. The nun wrote, "The rider was the famous Billy, the Kid!

The following year the Lincoln County War exploded into flames and Sister Blandina came to hear the name of Billy the Kid in association with it and falsely concluded that it was the same man she had known in Colorado. This is an example of her lack of knowledge about what went on about her for William Bonney's name appeared in the Santa Fe newspapers (under the names Henry McCarty, Henry Antrim, Kid Mc-Carty, Kid Antrim and William H. Bonney) on a regular basis yet she was unaware of this. The first time the name of William Bonney appeared in print was after March 18, 1878, when it was first written in the final letter of William Morton. All of the names Bonney was known by were used by all the New Mexico papers up until his death on July 14, 1881. Sister Blandina, unfortunately, was out of touch with the times.

On April 24, 1881, Sister Blandina wrote a letter to Sister Justina in Trinidad that one of her patients had been murdered by a man named Edward Kelly, a bartender in nearby Cerrillos. She said that Kelly was then in the Santa Fe jail along with her old friend Billy the Kid. She remarked that she would soon go down and visit them.

A month following, on May 16th, she again wrote Sister Justina and said she had gone to the jail where she had a chance to talk to Edward Kelly and that Billy the Kid was lodged in the same cell.

"I have just returned from the jail. The two prisoners were chained hands and feet, but the 'Kid' besides being cuffed hands and feet, was also fastened to the floor. You can imagine the extreme discomfort of the position. When I got into the prison cell and 'Billy' saw me, he said — as though we had met yesterday instead of four years ago — 'I wish I could place a chair for you sister.' At a glance I saw the contents of the prison. Two empty nail kegs, one empty soap box, one backless chair upon which sat the man who had shot our patient. After a few minute's talk the 'Kid' said to me 'Do what you can for Kelly,' pointing to the chair. 'This is his first offense and he was not himself when he did it. I'll get out of this: you will see, Sister."[11]

William H. Bonney was delivered to the Santa Fe jail on December 27, 1880, although the nun was not aware of this for the following three months. On March 29th Bonney was picked up by Tony Neis and Robert Olinger and taken to Mesilla for trial so he was not in the jail on Water Street when Sister Blandina arrived in late April or early May. If she had asked for Billy the Kid the jailer would have informed her that he was not there but, instead, she asked to see Edward Kelly and LeRoy happened to be in the same cell with him.

Further proof of the difference was that LeRoy was in a cell with Kelly with two nail kegs, a soap box and a chair while the records show that Garrett had Bonney placed alone in a cell, chained to the floor and without furnishings of any sort. Neither was there a window in his cell for Garrett was well aware of Bonney's penchant for discharging himself from jails on a "leg warrant." In fact, he almost escaped from the Santa Fe jail but was discovered in time. There was also a hole in the ceiling above his cell where the guards could look down and check on him from time to time.[12]

There is also some question about the May 16 date of Sister Blandina's letter for the Colorado papers reported that on May 12th Billy LeRoy and brother Sam had made an unsuccessful attempt to rob a stagecoach east of Del Norte, Colorado, and had been forced to outrun a posse to escape. On the day of her letter, May 16th, LeRoy, Sam and an unidentified bandit held up the Del Norte-Lake City stage 40 minutes outside of Clear Creek along the old Ute Trail.[13]

At exactly 8 p.m. the six-horse Barlow and Sanderson rig approached some moss-covered rocks near Antelope Springs with driver Joe McCormick in the boot. Beside him sat Frank Bartlett, an engineer for the Denver and Rio Grande Railroad. Three bandits stepped out on the trail and without warning fired three shots at McCormick and Bartlett. McCormick escaped the fusilade but one shot struck Bartlett in the thigh.

While Sam Pond held a rifle on the pair LeRoy, a small pistol clutched in his hand, climbed aboard the coach with the third bandit. They were seeking the strongbox but there was none. Instead they took a gold watch and $110 from Bartlett and tossed down five mail pouches to the ground. The stage was allowed to drive on and headed back to Clear Creek to report the robbery.

The Lake City telegraph informed Del Norte authorities that LeRoy was on the loose again and local citizens were angry at this latest outrage. A posse was quickly financed and the government posted a reward of $2,000 and local citizens matched this with a $400 reward. Sheriff Lew Armstrong headed the posse and M.G. Frost, Division Superintendent for the state line, turned over the facilities of the Barlow and Sanderson stage operation to Armstrong.

The posse could not start out until the following morning and arrived upon the scene to discover a fresh, three-inch snowfall had fallen during the night. The bandits' tracks were erased so they began riding around in ever-widening circles in an effort to cut their trail. A mile away from the scene they discovered the rifled mail sacks which had been cut open and discarded. The sacks had contained $1,286.57 and only $45 in cash.

Unknown to the posse at the time the three bandits were only two miles distant in the camp of surveyor W.H. Cochran and party. The bandits had been riding down the Ute Trail without looking up when they suddenly came upon Cochran's camp. They stopped and talked it over and when they realized that they had been spotted they rode on into camp. Cochran ordered the cook to feed the men and they ate quietly and quickly but kept glancing around as if watching for someone.

When Cochran stood up and announced that he had to post some mail at the Clear Creek station the bandits became very excited and made haste to depart. This aroused Cochran's suspicions. LeRoy made an offer to purchase Cochran's rifle but he declined.

Cochran waited until the trio had left before dispatching a man to the Clear Creek station to see if there was any news of wanted men and another man to Powderhorn station on the Cebolla side of the range to notify the stock tender to inform the authorities that something suspicious was going on. The next day Captain Burrows, John Ewing, Robert Shields, and Dr. F.G. Flourney came to the Cochran camp.

In the meantime Sheriff Armstrong had ridden to the opposite side of Lone Ridge to the Galloway ranch to see if the bandits might have gone in their direction or towards Baker Park. When Captain Burrows received Cochran's report he sent a rider to overtake Armstrong and return him to the Cochran camp.

The two parties met and discussed the situation. In the meantime two ranchers from Antelope Park named Dan Soward and M.G. Frost arrived to lend their assistance. The main body then moved two miles down the Ute Trail when they chanced to see a thin plume of smoke hanging over the distant trees. It was the smoke of the campfire. The posse approached the site with stealth and great care to discover a man standing with a rifle cradled in his arms beside the warming embers of a fire. He kept looking off into the distance toward the treeline as if awaiting the return of someone. He was totally unaware of their approach until Armstrong shouted for him to hold up his hands.

The startled man spun around and seeing the size of the posse decided discretion was the better part of valor and complied. He fit the description of one of the bandits and readily admitted that his name was Sam Pond and that he was one of the bandits. One outlaw had gone to Lake City for food while the other had headed toward a toll camp to try and buy a rifle.

It was evident that this was a poorly-planned and executed robbery for the bandits were totally lacking in the proper weaponry required for such a task. Sam Pond's hands were bound behind him and he was returned to Clear Creek station while Armstrong and Galloway remained hidden in the trees. They were certain the remaining outlaws would return. They didn't have to wait long.

An hour later a man rode out of the treeline in the direction of the little camp. He was not a cautious man for he did not even glance around the clearing before dismounting beside some bushes. The fact that Sam Pond was nowhere in sight apparently did not arouse any suspicions of danger in him. Once the horse was tied he finally glanced about as both lawmen stepped out and ordered him to throw up his hands. The man turned and raced for the trees some distance beyond. Though it was a 130 yard shot Armstrong took his time and the lead ball caught the fleeing man in the fleshy part of the calf of the left leg and he went down. He did not bother to regain his feet but continued crawling into the brush on his hands and knees.

The two lawmen did not follow him but shouted for him to come out and give himself up which he did moments later. It was Billy LeRoy.

The only weapon he had on his person was a small .38 caliber pistol which was quickly removed while he was lashed to a tree. Here he remained throughout the night while Armstrong and Galloway waited for the return of the third man but he never put in an appearance.

Billy and Sam were removed to Wagon Wheel Gap where John Murphy, the keeper of the station, told them that 200 angry Del Norte citizens were bent on lynching the prisoners and were on their way to intercept them. As it turned out only a small crowd of curious people were on hand at the station to greet them and to ask questions.

LeRoy, as Bonney had been in Las Vegas, was very talkative and answered all inquiries made to him and quickly admitted that Sam Pond was his brother. None of the money was found on them from the stage robbery for it had been given to the third member to buy food but he never returned. A piece of torn cloth was hastily wrapped around LeRoy's wounded leg and a makeshift bed was made on the floor for the men to sleep on. The first half of the night the two men were guarded by Siebard and Cleghorn and relieved for the final watch by Garner, Jackson and Jordan.

During the questioning Leroy sought to better his position by claiming that his first stage holdup had been committed only the previous fall in conjunction with a man from California whose name, unfortunately, he could not remember. As he spoke a sense of false bravado took over and soon, like all outlaws, he was bragging of his exploits. He claimed to have been broke and starving in Leadville and forced to steal pies from kitchen windows in order to survive. He also claimed to have stolen a shotgun from a Lake City sawmill earlier and had some kind of unexplained grudge against the government.

Sam admitted to using the alias of Silas Porter but lied when he claimed he had only been in the country for a short while. As the questioning progressed Sam broke down and admitted he had been the person that had fired upon the stagecoach the week before.

On May 21st the party departed for Del Norte and ate lunch at the Edwin Shaw ranch which was the mid-point of their journey. Armstrong sent scouts ahead to see that the road was clear before proceeding.

The LeRoys were delivered to the jail and locked in their cell at 11 p.m. that night. It wasn't until the next morning that Del Norte citizens were aware of their presence and ill feelings ran high. Many meetings were held about town in various saloons and Armstrong feared for the lives of his prisoners so had them guarded around the clock as protection. It proved to be of no value.

On May 23rd the LeRoys appeared before the court where they were tried and found guilty of the holdup of the Barlow and Sanderson stage. Both men were found to be guilty and Judge Hallett of the District Court sentenced them to ten years each at hard labor. They were destined never to serve their time. The brothers were returned to jail and guarded by Williard Cleghorn, John Ewing and George A. Seibard.

Now that the bandits were duly sentenced it was felt that perhaps the lynch feeling would gradually subside but it was not to be. At midnight of May 23rd the guards heard a knock at the jail door and a voice identified himself as Sheriff Armstrong. When the door was opened a lynch mob burst in and quickly overcame the guards before anyone could react. When the vigilantes unlocked the door to the LeRoy's cell neither man displayed the slightest trace of emotion or resistance but went willingly with their executioners. They were marched to a large tree a half-block west of the Del Norte railroad station.

While their feet and arms were being bound with wire and the hangman's rope placed about their necks they were asked whether they had any last words to say or not. Sam replied quietly that he did not but Billy chose to remain silent. Once this formality was out of the way both men were slowly hauled hand-over-hand into eternity. Their stiff bodies were left swaying in the cool spring breeze until sometime the following morning before being cut down. They were then propped up against the side of the railroad station and a photograph taken which clearly displayed the wire about their necks, wrists and ankles.

An inquest was quickly held over the corpses by coroner L.T. Holland who stated that their real names were Arthur and Sam Pond or Potter. Sam had the letters S.P. tatooed on a forearm but no one can be certain these were their given names. The were buried in lot 45A of the Del Norte Cemetery.

Only two articles have ever been discovered in New Mexico newspapers concerning the two men and each was unceremoniously tucked away in the territorial gossip column.

> Billy LeRoy, the stage robber of southern Colorado, and an ac-
> complice who is believed to have been his brother, paid the extreme
> penalty for crime at Del Norte on Sunday night. The executioners
> were an enraged, outraged people. [14]

The second and final article was orginally printed in the **Denver Republican** and reprinted in the **New Southwest & Herald.**

> The tragic end of Billy LeRoy, the stage robber, brings to mind a joke
> perpetrated at his expense by Judge Hallett of the United States
> Court. On calling up LeRoy for sentence, the judge asked him his
> age, and the prisoner responded gruffly, 'Twenty-three.' The judge
> then proceeded to sentence the prisoner to ten years in the peniten-
> tiary, adding, 'That will make your age just thirty-three when you are
> discharged — young enough to become a member of congress or an
> Indian agent.' Judge Hallett does not often indulge in sarcasm, but
> when he does it is effective. [15]

The first and original Billy the Kid was dead and his successor had but a month and a half left to live. Though LeRoy had operated over a seven year period and gained much notoriety in Colorado, William Bonney had a shorter span of three and a half years. Yet, for some unknown reason, future writers and historians would single Bonney out for immortality while LeRoy's name faded from the pages of history.

While Bonney was to become far more famous and his name a

household word known to every family and schoolchild, and while his memory is immortalized in film and the written word he will always remain a carbon copy of his namesake — a counterfeit Kid like the rest.

From July 14th, 1881 onward, the life of William Bonney would disappear into misconceptions, assumptions, misrepresentations and lies until little of the real man remained. Why do these things happen?

John W. Poe summed up the entire matter correctly when he said, "It seems too bad that people will circulate erroneous and false stories about this occurrence but I suppose it is one of the things that will have to be endured." [16]

NOTES
CHAPTER 7

1. Register of Prisoners Confined in the County Jail of Grant County, New Mexico, 1883. State Archives & Records Center, Santa Fe, New Mexico.
2. Ibid., 1884.
3. **Tascosa Pioneer,** date unknown.
4. **The Black Hills Trails,** by A.M. "Cap" Williard & Jesse Brown.
5. **Las Vegas Optic,** March 24, 1882. Both names appeared on a wanted poster.
6. Criminal Docket Book C, Sierra County, New Mexico. 1888.
7. Criminal Docket Book, 1888. Trinidad, Colorado, and arrest warrant.
8. **Thirty-Four,** Wednesday, January 22, 1879.
9. **Thirty-Four,** Wednesday, May 29, 1879.
10. **Arizona Star,** Nov. 19, 1887.
11. Sister Blandina's letter dated May 16, 1881.
12. **Santa Fe New Mexican,** January, 1881.
13. **Real West,** "They Died On Lonesome Road," by Jim Reilly by permission of his widow Stella A. Reilly. **New Southwest & Grant County Herald** and **The New Southwest & Herald,** June 4, 1881. Letter of Dean Hammond, owner of **The Del Norte Prospector** dated October 9, 1964.
14. **The New Southwest & Grant County Herald,** June 4, 1881, No. 26.
15. **New Southwest & Herald,** June 4, 1881.
16. Letter of John W. Poe to E.A. Brinstool of Los Angeles dated March 5, 1923. He was speaking of the folklore surrounding the life and death of William H. Bonney.

BIBLIOGRAPHIC SOURCES

GOVERNMENTAL OFFICES
Office of Ronald Reagan, President of the United States.
Office of Lyndon B. Johnson, President of the United States.
Edwin Mechem, U.S. Senator.
Manuel Lujan, U.S. Congressman.
Joseph M. Montoya, U.S. Senator.
Federal Archives & Records Center. General Services Administration Center. Laguna Niguel, California.
Federal Records Center, St. Louis, Missouri. Reference Service Branch.
General Services Administration. Retired Army Records Center.
National Archives & Records Center, Central Research Room Branch.
National Archives & Records Center, General Services Administration.
National Archives Trust Fund Board, NNMS. Washington, D.C.
Personal Census Service Branch.
U.S. Department of Immigration in Washington, D.C. & El Paso, Texas.
U.S. Department of Commerce, Bureau of the Census. Pittsburgh, Kansas.
U.S. Department of Justice, Immigration & Naturalization Service, Ship manifest of the **Devonshire,** April 10, 1846.

FOREIGN
Consulate General of Ireland. C.V. Whelan, Consul General of Ireland in San Francisco, California.
National Library of Ireland. Alf Mac Lochlainn, Asst. Keeper of Manuscripts in Dublin, Ireland.

NEWSPAPERS
Albuquerque Journal, August 4, 1963.
Albuquerque Review, May 1880.
Albuquerque Tribune, June 21, 1960.
Advance, April-May, 1880.
Arizona Weekly Star, August 23, 1877.
Cimarron News & Press, April 11, 1878.
Daily New Mexican, January 1877-December 1881 conculsive.
Dallas Morning News, June 28, 1928.
Dallas Weekly, July 21, 1881.
Denver Post, April 1, 1891.
Eddy Argus, January 24, 1891.
Grant County Herald, 1874-1881 conclusive.
Indianapolis Star, June 24, 1956.
Laredo Times, August 10, 1881.
Las Cruces **Thirty Four,** 1878-1879 conclusive.
Las Vegas Gazette, 1877-1881 conclusive.
Las Vegas Optic, 1877-1881 conclusive.

Lincoln County Leader, January 15, 1890.

Mesilla Independent, 1878-1881 conclusive.

Mesilla Semi-Weekly, 1880-1881 conclusive.

New York Herald, July-September 1862.

New York Sun, July 22, 1881.

New York Times, January 1850-December 1859 conclusive; August-September 1862; September-November 1876; July-August 1881; plus selected issues.

Philadelphia Times, July 20, 1881.

Santa Fe New Mexican, 1877-1881; September 5, 1931; December 9, 1931.

The Citizen, August 25, 1877.

The New Southwest & Herald, 1880-1881 conclusive.

The Southwesterner, August 1962; June 1963.

The Sun, September 10, 1876.

The Territorian, 1961-1963 conclusive.

The World, September 10, 1876.

Tombstone Epitaph, November 18, 1881.

MAGAZINES

Frontier Times, July 1, 1943.

The West, "Montana's Bloodiest Day," by Joe Koller.

True West, "The Secret Life of Billy the Kid," by Don Cline. April 1984.

MICROFILM

1860 Arizona Census Index & microfilm.

1870 Arizona Census Index & microfilm.

1880 Arizona Census Index & microfilm.

1820 Indiana.

1830 Indiana.

1840 Indiana.

1850 Indiana.

1860 Indiana.

1870 Indiana.

1860 Kansas.

1870 Kansas.

1850 New York City — Wards 1,2,3,4 in New York & Brooklyn.

1860 New York City — Wards 1,2,3,4, in New York and Wards 3,4 in Brooklyn.

1870 New York City — second enumeration for Wards 2,3,4.

1870 New Mexico.

1875 New Mexico — territorial census.

1880 New Mexico.

1890 New Mexico.

1900 New Mexico.

1910 New Mexico.

1880 Texas — Bexas, Oldham, Potter, Wichita, Wheeler, Willbarger and Wood Counties.

1800 Ohio.

1800 Pennsylvania.

Annals of Old Fort Cummings, Apache Indian Wars. Roll 500-30.

Camp Grant Post Returns, March 1877-November 1877.

Official Records of The Union and Confederate Armies 1861-1865 including index listing of all participants in the war.

Texas Ranger Service Records 1847-1900.

COUNTIES SEARCHED

Arizona — Graham and Pima.

Texas — Clay, El Paso, Gray, Pecos, Moore, Potter, Reeves, Wheeler, and Wichita Counties.

New York — Kings County.

Kansas — Butler, Sedwick, Shawnee Counties.

New Mexico — Chaves, Colfax, Dona Ana, Grant, Lincoln, San Miguel, Santa Fe, Sierra and Socorro Counties.

Indiana — Madison, Marion Counties including Indianapolis.

Ohio — Columbiana and Delaware Counties.

REAL ESTATE INDEX RECORDS

Bernalillo County, New Mexico.

Chaves County, New Mexico.

Colfax County, New Mexico.

Curry County, New Mexico.

Eddy County, New Mexico.

El Paso County, Texas.

Grant County, New Mexico.

Lincoln County, New Mexico.

Madison County, Indiana.

Marion County, Indiana.

San Miguel County, New Mexico.

Santa Fe County, New Mexico.

Sedgwick County, Kansas.

Socorro County, New Mexico.

DEATH RECORDS

Arizona Death Records.

Chaves County, New Mexico.

Dona Ana County, New Mexico.

El Paso County, Texas.

Grant County, New Mexico.

Kings County, New York.

Lincoln County, New Mexico.

Madion County, Indiana.

Marion County, Indiana.

Montgomery County, Ohio.
San Miguel County, New Mexico.
Santa Fe County, New Mexico.
Socorro County, New Mexico.
Texas — various counties.

CITY OFFICES AND LIBRARIES
Amarillo Municipal Library.
Anderson Chamber of Commerce. Anderson, Indiana.
Bureau of Vital Statistics. Denver, Colorado.
City of Chicago, Department of Police files.
City of Denver Municipal Library.
City of Trinidad, Colorado. Department of Police files.
Colorado Historical Society.
Department of Library, Archives and Public Records. Phoenix, Arizona.
El Paso Municipal Library.
Lubbock Municipal Library.
Midland Municipal Library & Nita Stewart Haley Memorial Library.
Odessa Public Library.
New York City: County Coroner's Records 1877. Municipal Archives, Dept. of Records & Information Services.
New York City: Police Museum, Detective Thomas Krant, Police Historian & Curator of Police Museum NYPD.
New York City: Office of the Chief Medical Examiner.
New York City: The Children's Aid Society.
New York Hospital, Medical Information Department.
New York City: Historical Society.
New York City Divorce Records.
New York City Municipal Library.
New York City public schools records.
New York City: Department of Health, Borough Register.
New York City: County Clerk's Office.
New York City: Bureau of Health, Bureau of Records & Statistics.
New York City: Municipal Archives & Records Center.
New York City: Lyons, New York, Chamber of Commerce for Wayne County.
New York City: Human Resources Division. Services for Children, Division of Adoption and Foster Care Services.

STATE OFFICES
Division of Vital Statistics, New Mexico Department of Public Health. Santa Fe, New Mexico.
New Mexico Department of Public Health.
State Museum, Lincoln, New Mexico.
State Library, Western History Department. Santa Fe, New Mexico.
University of New Mexico, Coronado Room. Albuquerque, New Mexico.

University of Texas at El Paso, Archives Division. El Paso, Texas.

COUNTY OFFICES & COURTS

Clerk of the Supreme Court, New York City.

Clerk — General Services & Superior Court, New York City.

County Recorder, Hall of Records, Los Angeles, California.

County Health Department & County Recorder's Office. San Luis Obispo, California.

County Clerk's Office, New Mexico: Bernalillo, Colfax, Chaves, Curry, DeBaca, Eddy, Guadalupe, Lincoln, Otero, Roosevelt, Santa Fe, Sierra Counties.

OTHER

Colorado — County Clerk's Office, Conejos Colorado; Las Animas County Health Department. Bureau of Vital Statistics. Las Animas County. Trinidad, Colorado.

Kansas — Montgomery & Sedgwick Counties.

Illinois — Cook and St. Clair Counties.

New York — Kings County.

DISTRICT COURTS

Arizona — Graham and Pinal Counties.

Colorado — Las Animas County.

New Mexico — Bernalillo, Chaves, Colfax, Curry, DeBaca, Dona Ana, Eddy, Grant, Lea, Lincoln, Luna, Roosevelt, San Miguel, Quay, Sierra and Socorro Counties.

New York — Kings County.

Texas — El Paso, Greene, Pecos, Potter Counties.

MISCELLANEOUS

Adjutant General's Files in State Library in Austin, Texas.

Arizona Historical Society in Tucson, Arizona.

Ash Upson letters in Santa Fe at State Records & Archives Center.

Brands Book. Lincoln County 1869-1879.

Brands Book. Dona Ana County 1875-1900.

Cash Receipt Books, Dona Ana County.

Cash Receipts Books, Lincoln County.

Chauncey O. Truesdell letter of Sept. 29, 1950, and Robert N. Mullin interview January 9, 1952.

City Directories — Albuquerque 1883; El Paso 1912-1923; Roswell 1915-1957; Las Vegas 1881-1932; Indianapolis 1860-1872; Los Angeles 1920-1924; New York 1850-1865; Wichita 1870.

Civil Docket Books — Bernalillo, Chaves, Colfax, Curry, DeBaca, El Paso, Grant, Dona Ana, Pima, Pinal, San Miguel Counties.

Chaves County Tax Rolls, 1920. Also assessor's rolls.

Godfrey Gauss affidavit in **Lincoln County Leader**, Jan. 15, 1890.

Governor Lew Wallace papers in State Records & Archives Center in Santa Fe, New Mexico, on microfilm.

Grant County assessment rolls 1885 & 1887.

Johnson Memorial Mortuary in Las Vegas, New Mexico. Also Gonzales Funeral Home in Las Vegas, New Mexico.

Lt. John G. Bourke's original field reports in bound form in the Coronado Room of the University of New Mexico. 1872-1877.

Lincoln County Commissioner's Minutes Books 1877-1881.

Panhandle Plains Historical Museum in Canyon, Texas.

Penitentiary of New Mexico records, Santa Fe, New Mexico.

Presbyterian Historical Society records.

U.S. Presbyterian Ministerial Directory.

Register of Prisoners Confined to the Grant County Jail of Grant County 1877-1895.

Sandra Crittenden — information on Ed Moulton of Silver City.

State Bar of New Mexico.

San Miguel County Justice of the Peace Inquest Book No. 1.

MINING RECORDS

General Index to Lode Records 1 & 16. Socorro County.

General Index to Lode Records B. Socorro County.

Deed & Mining Records Book K & V. Socorro County.

Grant County Mining Records.

Mining Deeds 1881-1893. Socorro County.

Mining Records & Proof of Labor 1881-1923. Socorro County.

INDIANA RECORDS

Indiana Birth Records.

Indiana Death Records.

Indiana Real Estate Records.

Indiana State Library & Genealogy Division.

OTHER

Catholic Church Birth & Marriage records in Lincoln and San Miguel Counties.

Pojoaque Valley School records. Superintendent's Office.

REA Express, San Francisco, California.

Robert Olinger papers in Lincoln County courthouse files.

St. Rita's Catholic Church records in Carrizozo, New Mexico.

Warrants records of Lincoln County 1875-1881.

Wells Fargo Bank records. San Francisco, California.

PEOPLE

A.R. Mitchell, curator of the Baca House Museum in Trinidad, Colorado.

Belle Wilson, curator of the Lincoln Museum in Lincoln, New Mexico.

C.G. Silva of Fort Sumner, New Mexico.

Gertrude Graham Butler of Bard, New Mexico.

Ray Turner of Channing, Texas.

Roy Brady, great-great-great grandson of Sheriff William Brady.

NOTE: Many sources have not been listed because of the amount over a 22 year period or were simply left out by mistake. Sources searched but nothing found were not listed.

BOOKS

Accelerated Indexing Systems Inc., **Index to Ohio Tax Lists 1800-1810.** Dana Press, Bountiful, Utah, 1977.

Beard, Mrs. Jane, **Births, Deaths, & Marriages From El Paso Newspapers Through 1885.** Southern Historical Press, El Paso, Texas, 1982.

Bell, Carol Willsey, **Ohio Wills and Estates To 1850: An Index.** Bell Books, Youngstown, Ohio, 1981.

Boettcher, Joe, **Las Vegas In The 1880's, From November 1879-November 1880,** typed manuscript, Las Vegas, New Mexico, no date.

Burke's Genealogical And Heraldic History of Peerage Baronetage Knightage 1826, Shaw Publishing Company, London, England, 1954 reprint.

C. de Baca, Maria Elba, **Las Vegas In The 1880's,** typed manuscript, Las Vegas, New Mexico, no date.

Clemens, William Montgomery, **American Marriage Records Before 1699,** Genealogical Publishing Co., Baltimore, Maryland, 1967.

Coe, George, **Frontier Fighter,** University of New Mexico Press, Albuquerque, New Mexico, 1951.

Corn, Mrs. Robert Irwin, **New Mexico Cemetery Records,** typed manuscript, 1958.

Ellis, Eilish, **Emigrants From Ireland 1847-1852,** Genealogical Publishing Co., Baltimore, Maryland, 1978.

Evetts, J. Haley, **Charles Goodnight – Cowman and Plainsman,** University of Oklahoma Press, Norman, Oklahoma, 1949.

_____, **The XIT Ranch,** University of Oklahoma Press, Norman, Oklahoma, 1953.

Forkner, John L., & Dyson, Byron H., **Historical Sketches and Reminiscences of Madison County, Indiana,** Wilson, Humphreys & Co., Logansport, Indiana, 1897.

Fox, Richard K., **Billy LeRoy, The Colorado Bandit, Or, The King of American Highmen,** Police Gazette, New York, 1881.

Garrett, Patrick, **The Authentic Life of Billy the Kid,** University of Oklahoma Press, Norman, Oklahoma, 1954.

Genealogical Publishing Co., **List of Pensioners on the Roll 1883, Vol. 1, 1-5,** Baltimore, Maryland, 1970.

_____, **The Famine Immigrants. Lists of Irish Immigrants Coming In At the Port of New York 1846-1851, Vols. 1-4,** Baltimore, Maryland, 1983.

_____, **Blackford County, Indiana, Tract Book 1831-1853**, Selby Publishing Co., Indiana, no date.

Gonzales, Emilia, **Las Vegas In 1879**, typed manuscript, Las Vegas, New Mexico, no date.

Gregory, Winifred, **American Newspapers 1821-1936**, Biographical Society of America, Kraus reprint, New York, 1967,

Heiss, Willard, **Indiana Source Book**, Indiana Historical Society, Indianapolis, Indiana, 1977.

_____, **Warren County-Ohio-Marriage Records 1834-1854**, Private printing, Indianapolis, Indiana, 1977.

Henshaw, William Wade, **Encyclopedia of Amercian Quaker Genealogy** (various states), Genealogical Publishing Co., Baltimore, Maryland, 1973.

History of Madison County, Indiana 1820-1874, A Reproduction of Unigraphic Inc., Indiana, 1970.

Hoosier Journal of Ancestry, Private printing, Little York, Indiana, 1983.

Lists of Private Claims, compiled by the House of Representatives, Balitmore, Maryland, 1890.

Hoyt, Dr. Henry F., **Frontier Doctor**, Houghton-Mifflin Co., Cambridge, Mass., 1929.

Encyclopedia of American Quaker Genealogy, (Indiana, Ohio, Illinois, Pennsylvania & Kansas), Indiana Historical Society, Indianapolis, Indiana, 1984.

Indiana Source Book I, Henry and Delaware Counties, Indiana, Marriages 1827-1841, Indiana Historical Society, Indianpolis, Indiana, 1979.

Indiana Source Book I, Marion County, Indiana, Marriages, 1822-1830, Indiana Historical Society, Indianpolis, Indiana, 1977.

Keleher, William, A., **Violence In Lincoln County**, University of New Mexico Press, Albuquerque, New Mexico, 1957.

_____, **The Fabulous Frontier**, University of New Mexico Press, Albuquerque, New Mexico, 1962.

Lavash, Donald R., **Sheriff William Brady, Tragic Hero of the Lincoln County War**, Sunstone Press, Santa Fe, New Mexico, 1986.

Madison County Historical Society, **History of Madison County, Illinois**, W.R. Brink & Co., Edwardsville, Illinois, 1882.

McCarty, John L., **Maverick Town, The Story of Old Tascosa**, University of Oklahoma Press, Norman, Oklahoma, 1946.

Mullin, Robert N., **The Boyhood of Billy the Kid**, Western Press, El Paso, Texas, 1963.

Metz, Leon C., **Pat Garrett, The Story of a Western Lawman**, University of Oklahoma Press, Norman, Oklahoma, 1973.

O'Connor, Richard, **Pat Garrett**, Doubleday, New York, 1960.

Pennsylvania Vital Records, Genealogical Publishing Co., Baltimore, Maryland, 1978.

Perrigo, Lynn, **Las Vegas in the 1880's**, typed manuscript, Las Vegas, New Mexico, no date.

Powell, Esther Weygandt, **The Index to Early Ohio Tax Records 1800-1810**, Unincorporated Indexes, Akron, Ohio, 1895.

Poe, John W., **Billy the Kid,** 2nd Edition, Frontier Press, Texas, 1919.

Porter, Millie, **Memory Cups of Panhandle Pioneers,** Clarendon Press, Clarendon, Texas, 1945.

Rickards, Colin, **Sheriff Pat Garrett's Last Days,** Sunstone Press, Santa Fe, New Mexico, 1986.

Scanland, John Milton, **Life of Pat Garrett and the Taming of the Border Outlaw,** Southwestern, El Paso, Texas, 1952.

Scott, Kenneth, **Abstracts From Franklin's Pennsylvania Gazette 1728-1940,** Genealogical Publishing Co., Baltimore, Maryland, 1975.

Scott, Col. Robert N., **Official Records of the Union and Confederate Armies 1861-1865,** and **Addition & Corrections Series,** Government Printing Office, Washington, D.C., 1889.

Seagle, Sister Blandina, **At the End of the Santa Fe Trail,** Bruce Publishing Co., Milwaukee, Wisconsin, 1948.

Siringo, Charles, **Riata and Spurs,** Houghton-Mifflin Co., New York, 1927.

————, **History of Billy the Kid,** Steck Publishing Co., Santa Fe, New Mexico, 1920.

Smith, Clifford N., **Federal Land Series,** American Library Association, 1972.

Sullivan, Dulcie, **The LS Brand,** University of Texas Press, Austin, Texas, 1968.

Ross, Charles P. & Rouse, T.C., **Official Early-Day History of Willbarger County, Vernon Daily Record,** Vernon, Texas, 1933.

Topeka Genealogical Society, **Kansas Pioneers,** Topeka, Kansas, 1976.

Turner, Ida Marie & Vickery, Adele W., **Marriages of Wood County, Texas, 1879-1903,** Private printing, Mineola, Texas, 1971.

Twitchell, Ralph Emerson, **Leading Facts of New Mexico History,** Torch Press, Cedar Rapids, Iowa, 1911.

Williams, Clayton W., **Texas' Last Frontier: Fort Stockton & Trans Pecos 1861-1895,** Texas A & M University Press, Bryan, Texas, 1902.

Williams, Oscar W., **Pioneer Surveyor — Frontier Lawyer,** Texas Western College, El Paso, Texas, 1966.

INDEX

Allison, Charles Leon: 87
Antrim, Catherine: 11, 15-17, 19-21, 23, 25-30, 36
Antrim family: 23-25, 28
Antrim, Henry SEE: Billy the Kid
Antrim, James Madison: 23-25
Antrim, William H.: 17-19, 23-25, 27-32, 34-38, 46, 90
Apaches: 47-49
Armijo, Perfecto: 88-90
Armstrong, Lew: 127-129
Atkins, John: 74

Bailey, G.W.: 29
Baker, Frank: 55-56, 62-64
Bartlett, Frank: 126
Battle of the O.K. Corral, Tombstone, AZ: 121
Baylor, Charles: 29
Becalo, Bito: 70
Beckwith, John: 104-105
Beckwith, Robert: 68-70
Bell, James W.: 73, 84, 104-106
Bernstein, Morris: 26-27
Billy the Kid: 11-16, 18, 21, 23, 26-42, 46-53, 55-64, 66-80, 83-91, 103-107, 109-117, 119-122, 124-126, 128, 130-131
Black, Robert: 34
Blandina, Sister: 123-126
Bonner, Billy: 122
Bonney, William H. SEE: Billy the Kid
Bottom, Charles: 29
Bourke, John G.: 49
Bowdre, Charlie: 60, 63-64, 77-80, 87, 91, 122
Bowdre, Manuela: 78
Bowdre, Mrs. Charlie: 86-87
Brady, William: 57, 64-69, 72-73, 86, 104-105
Brazil, Wayne: 113
Brewer, Dick: 60, 63

Bristol, Warren: 65
Brown, Henry: 63, 72
Brown, Mrs. R.H.: 13
Brown, Robert H.: 29
Brown, Sarah: 27-29, 32, 34
Burrows, Captain: 127

Cahill, Frank P.: 35, 46, 48-53, 73
Cahill, John ("Windy"): 49
Camp Grant: 47-53
Campbell, William: 70, 83-84
Casey, Mary Richards (Mrs. Daniel): 29, 31, 34, 111
Catron, Thomas B.: 60
Chambers, Lon: 76
Chapman, H.S. 70, 83-84
Chisum, Finian: 111-112
Chisum, John: 59-61, 65, 67-69, 111
Chung, Sam: 32
Claiborne, William F.: 121
Clanton, Ike: 121
Cleghorn, Williard: 129
Cochran, W.H.: 127
Coe, George: 13, 58-59, 67
Coglan, Pat: 76
Coleman, Charles: 55
Compton, Charles E.: 51-53
Cone, John: 71
Conner, Anthony B.: 31
Cook, Henry J.: 25
Cook, Samuel: 86
Corbett, Samuel R.: 70
Cornelius, William: 120
Crawford, Edith L.: 27
Cunningham, Eugene: 29
Currington, Jim: 110

Daggett, Thomas F.: 123
Dedrick brothers: 76
Dobbs, G.H. ("Kid"): 72, 76-77, 122
Dobie, J. Frank: 17
Dolan, Caroline: 86

Dolan, James J.: 26, 59-61, 69-70,
    83-84, 86
Doss, Sam: 58
Dwire, Matthew: 38, 41-42
Dwyer, John: 15, 17, 23, 37-39, 46
Dyer, Mrs.: 34

Earp, Morgan: 121
Earp, Virgil: 121
Earp, Wyatt: 121
Easton, David M.: 60
Ellis, Bob: 106-107
Ellis, Isaac: 70
Evans, Jesse: 55-57, 59, 70, 73-75,
    79, 83-84
Ewing, John: 127, 129

Fish, N.W.W.: 106
Fizpatrick, George: 103
Flourney, F.G.: 127
Foley, John: 52
Fountain, A.J.: 108
French, James: 63, 66-67
Frost, M.G.: 127
Fulton, Maurice G.: 28, 63
Fulton, Pete: 119

Gage, Laura: 29
Garcia, Abrana: 87
Garcia, Pantaleon: 60
Garrett, Patrick Floyd (Pat): 12-14,
    36, 46, 58-60, 67, 75-79, 90,
    103-106, 112-116, 126
Gaston, Charity Ann: 26
Gauss, Godrey: 106-107
Gildersleeve, Charles H.: 28
Givens, Isaac: 32
Glennon, Patience (Casey): 34
Gough, John B. ("Catfish Kid"):
    119-120
Graham, William Henry: 59-60, 63
Grant, Joe: 111-112
Greathouse, Jim: 76
Gutierrez, Celsa: 114-116
Gutierrez, Sabinal: 113-115

Hall, Lee: 76
Hamer, John: 123
Henry, Dutch: 71, 75-76
Hill, Tom: 55-56
Hindeman, George: 66, 73, 104
Hoggins, Luther D.: 58
Holland, L.T.: 130
Holliday, John ("Doc"): 85-86, 121
Holson, Mrs. T.W.: 34
Holt, George W.: 35
Horn, Lonny: 58
Howard, G.J.: 71
Hoyt, Henry F.: 71-72, 85, 90, 105

Irving, G.W.: 106

James, Frank: 83-85
James, Jesse: 83-85
Jaramillo, Adelaide: 28
Jones, Heiskell, 57
Jones, John A.: 104-105

Keleher, William A.: 28
Kelly, Edward: 125-126
Kelly, John: 39
Kinney, John W.: 55-56
Kinney, Thomas K. ("Kip"): 113, 115
Knight, Mary Richards: 34
Knight, Sarah Ann: 31, 34

Laughlin, N.B.: 106
Lavash, Don: 57
Lea, Joseph C. 13, 103, 109
Le Bel, Zoel: 52
LeRoy, Billy: 122-130
LeRoy, Sam SEE: Pond, Sam
Leslie, Frank ("Buckskin Frank"):
    121
Lesnett, A.E.: 27
Long, John: 66
Lincoln County War: 13, 56, 60-61,
    68-69, 86, 124-125
Lyons, Mrs. Thomas SEE:
    Gage, Laura

McCarty, Catherine SEE:
  Antrim, Catherine
McCarty, Catherine, of Indianapolis: 24-25
McCarty, Edward: 14, 37, 39-40, 46
McCarty, Henry SEE: Billy the Kid
McCarty, Joseph (Joe): 11, 14, 16, 26, 29-30, 35-40, 46, 90, 110
McCarty, Michael Henry: 15-17
McCarty, William: 18-19
McCloskey, William: 63-64
McCormick, Joe: 126
McDaniels, James: 50, 55-57
McFarland, D.F.: 26
McLowery, Frank: 121
McLowery, Tom: 121
McMasters, James E.: 71
McNabb, Frank: 63-64
McSween, Alexander: 13, 56, 58, 61-62, 64-65, 67-70, 83
McSween, Sue: 58, 61-62, 67, 70, 83
Magan, Richard F.: 39
Marrian, Lawrence: 90
Marshall, H.H.: 63
Martinez, Anatascio: 26
Mason, Barney: 110, 113
Matthews, Billy: 66-67
Maxwell, Deluvina: 58, 116-117
Maxwell, Lucien B.: 28, 58
Maxwell, Odilia: 58
Maxwell, Paulita: 58, 87, 114-115
Maxwell, Pete: 58-59, 110, 113-116
Mazzanovich, Anton: 52
Mechem, Edwin: 19
Middleton, John: 63, 72
Montoya, Alexander: 87
Montoya, Juana: 87
Moore, Thomas: 38-42, 73
Moore, Winfield Scott: 85
Moorehead, A.H.: 33
Morris, Harvey: 68-70
Morton, William: 62-64
Mouton, Ed: 29, 34-37, 46, 90
Mouton, Sarah: 37
Mullin, Robert N.: 27-30, 32, 35
Munns, Charles N.: 25

Murphy, John: 128
Murphy, Lawrence G.: 26, 59-61, 86
Myers, S.D.: 106

Neis, Tony: 90, 104-105, 126
Nevill, Charles L.: 74
Nolan, Frederick: 61

O'Callon, "Kentuck": 122
O'Folliard, Tom: 60, 70, 77-78, 83
Olinger, Robert: 73, 90, 104-109, 126
On The Border With Crook: 49
Osage Trust Lands: 23
Osborn, W.J.: 51, 53
Otero, Miguel A.: 13, 67

Parmer, Mrs. Allen: 84
Patron, Juana Montoya SEE:
  Montoya, Juana
Peppin, George: 66
Perry, Sam: 55-56
Pickett, Thomas: 86
Pierce, Milo: 105
Poe, John W.: 75-76, 113-116, 131
Pond, Arthur SEE: LeRoy, Billy
Pond, Sam: 122, 125-126, 128-130
Porter, Silas SEE: Pond, Sam
Presbyterian School,
  Santa Fe, NM: 26

Rasch, Phil: 28
Reasor, Charles: 72, 76-77
Regulators, The: 62-66, 68-70
Reich, Betty: 29
Richards, Mary Ann SEE:
  Casey, Mary Richards
Rinehart, Ira J.: 71
Rinehart, Irvin: 71
Roberts, Andrew ("Buckshot"): 104-105
Romero, Casmero: 71
Romero, Vicente: 70
Rudabaugh, Dave: 19, 73, 79-80, 103
Rudolph, Milnor: 114
Runte, Henry: 48
Ryan, Henry: 56

Ryan, Peter: 39

Salazar, Ygenio: 107
Schurz, Carl: 105
Scurlock, J.G. ("Doc"): 63, 70, 109
Seibard, George A.: 129
Selman, John: 71, 75-76
Shaefer, George: 32
Sherman, John: 109
Shield, Mrs. Elizabeth: 61
Shields, Robert; 127
Silva, Jesus: 112, 116
Silva, Jose D.: 103-104
Siringo, Charlie: 71, 77, 86-87
Slaughter, John: 59, 84
Smith, Gilbert C.: 52
Smith, Samuel: 60, 63
Sopris, Eldridge: 58
Soward, Dan: 127
Sperling, Charles: 74
Sperling, Frank: 74
Spiegelberg Brothers Store, Santa Fe:
    26-27
Starr, Henry: 120-121
Stewart, Frank: 76-77
Stoudenmire, Dallas: 107
Sullivan, T.: 48
Sun, Charlie: 32, 35-36
Swingle, Kid: 122

Taylor, Dan L.: 58
Taylor, Manuel: 32-33
Texas Jack: 84
Torrey, Ellsworth: 73, 76
Truesdell, Chauncey O.: 27, 33-35, 47
Truesdell family: 35
Tunstall, John: 60-62, 70

Upson, Marshall Ashmun: 12-14,
    17-18, 27, 34, 36-37, 63-64, 83

Vivian, May: 123

Waite, Fred: 63, 72
Wallace, Lew: 28, 69, 83-84, 105, 120
Webb, J.J.: 85

Webb, Robert G.: 39
Webster, J.: 29
White, Charlie: 85
Whitehill, Harry: 31
Whitehill, Harvey: 31-34, 36
Whittacer, James: 55-56
Whittaker, James SEE:
    Whittacer, James
Widenman, Robert A.: 60
Williams, Alexander: 39-42
William, O.W.: 106
Wilson, John B. ("Squire"): 62, 67,
    70, 88-89
Wilson, William: 120-121
Wilson, William H. ("Kid"): 63, 86,
    120
Winnie, Hank: 120
Wood, Miles Leslie: 50, 52-53
Wooten, Uncle Dick: 124
Wyeth, J.: 106

Yerby, Florentina: 88
Yerby, Nasaria: 87-88
Yerby, Tomas: 87-88
Younger brothers: 84-85

Zamora, Frank: 68-70